How to Build
SOCIAL
SCIENCE
THEORIES

Dedicated to. . .

F. Scott Sherman
Elaine F. Tankard
L. Richard Scroggins

How to Build SOCIAL SCIENCE THEORIES

Pamela J. Shoemaker
Syracuse University

James William Tankard, Jr.
University of Texas, Austin

Dominic L. Lasorsa
University of Texas, Austin

SAGE Publications
International Educational and Professional Publisher
Thousand Oaks ■ London ■ New Delhi

For information:

 Sage Publications, Inc.
2455 Teller Road
Thousand Oaks, California 91320
E-mail: order@sagepub.com

Sage Publications Ltd.
6 Bonhill Street
London EC2A 4PU
United Kingdom

Sage Publications India Pvt. Ltd.
B-42, Panchsheel Enclave
Post Box 4109
New Delhi 110 017 India

Printed in the United States of America

Library of Congress Cataloging-in-Publication Data

Shoemaker, Pamela J.
How to build social science theories / by Pamela J. Shoemaker, James William Tankard, Jr., Dominic L. Lasorsa ; foreword by Jerald Hage.
    p. cm.
Includes bibliographical references and index.
ISBN 0-7619-2666-6 — ISBN 0-7619-2667-4 (paper))
    1. Sociology-Methodology. 2. Social sciences-Methodology.
I. Tankard, James W. II. Lasorsa, Dominic L. III. Title.
HM585.S52 2004
300´.1—dc22

                                                    2003016653
Printed on acid-free paper.

          06   07   08   09   10   9   8   7   6   5   4   3   2

Acquiring Editor:	Margaret H. Seawell
Editorial Assistant:	Alicia Carter
Production Editor:	Claudia A. Hoffman
Copy Editor:	Elisabeth Magnus
Typesetter:	C&M Digitals (P) Ltd.
Indexer:	Sylvia Coates

Contents

Preface

One of us (Tankard) was teaching at the University of Wisconsin in 1970-71 when two graduate students, Robert Krull and James Watt, mentioned an exciting course they were taking from a sociology professor named Jerald Hage. The course dealt with theory building in sociology, and the students said Hage had just written his own text for the course and distributed it to the class in mimeographed form. Tankard showed interest in seeing the document, and Krull and Watt obtained a copy for him. It was 220 mimeographed pages, and the figures were drawn by hand. The title of the manuscript was *Techniques and Problems of Theory Construction*. The manuscript was not always easy reading, with examples taken primarily from sociology, but it dealt with the important matter of theory building in a more systematic and comprehensive way than anything else that was around.

In 1972, the manuscript was published by John Wiley & Sons under the title *Techniques and Problems of Theory Construction in Sociology*. Tankard, who was teaching theory and research methods at the University of Texas, began assigning chapters in graduate seminars. Despite a few student complaints about the difficulty of the material, he continued to assign chapters from the Hage book for years because the ideas were so important and useful.

Another of us (Shoemaker) remembers going through graduate classes at the University of Wisconsin in which theory building and testing were discussed and expecting to see an example of a theory with all its various parts. She discovered that there weren't any—social science theories tend to be spread in a nonsystematic way across many articles and books. This was the beginning of her interest in theory building. Shoemaker came to the University of Texas to teach in 1982 and began assigning chapters from the Hage book, which she knew about from her graduate courses at Wisconsin. The Hage "system" played a major role in the development of her dissertation at

Wisconsin, causing her for the first time to systematically provide theoretical and operational definitions for all concepts, along with theoretical and operational linkages for all hypotheses. At Texas, she required the book in her graduate theory classes until it went out of print. The students complained at the time about how difficult the book was to read and comprehend, but for years later, those same scholars said again and again how important the book ultimately was to their research programs.

In the spring of 1981, another of us (Lasorsa) was a master's student in a communication theory course taught by Tankard and received his first exposure to the Hage book. His initial reaction was typical of many students faced with Hage for the first time, reading Chapter 1 on theoretical statements and trying to digest it all: "Specific nonvariables? Primitive terms? Discrepancy variables? Do I really need to know this stuff?" The teacher tried his best to convince the student that if he wanted to learn how to construct theory, then, yes, he probably did need to know this stuff. Lasorsa accepted Tankard's word and went on to become a teacher himself. Now he, too, tries to instruct others in the ways of Hage.

The models chapter of this book includes a model of the cultivation process that Lasorsa first began developing while a student in Tankard's communication theory seminar.

One of the shortcomings of the Hage book that became noticeable in the 1980s was that it dealt mostly with theoretical statements relating two variables. This limitation prompted Tankard to write a paper titled "Beyond Hage: Building Communication Theory by Exploring Three-Variable Relationships," which was presented at an international conference in Montreal in 1987. Shoemaker began using this paper in seminars along with the Hage readings and also added some figures that helped in the visualizing of three-variable relationships.

Lasorsa finished his master's degree and went to study for a doctorate at Stanford. He returned to Texas to teach in 1986. At this point, all three of us were at the University of Texas, teaching courses in social science research methods and communication theory. We began talking about writing our own book on theory building. The book would update and extend some of Hage's thinking but would also explore new areas, such as three- and four-variable relationships and the role of creativity in theory building. Another factor motivating us was that, at a certain point, the Hage volume went out of print. A recent search of amazon.com found a used copy of Hage's book for sale for $126.96.

In 1989, the three of us began meeting for lunch at Les Amis, a sidewalk café (now replaced by a Starbucks) a block away from the university, and discussing theory building. After a meeting or two, we gave ourselves the assignment of each writing every 2 weeks a five-page essay on any aspect of theory building that interested us. We also came up with our first outline for a book dealing with theory building.

In 1991, Shoemaker left the University of Texas to become an administrator at Ohio State University, and the theory-building project was shelved for a while. When Shoemaker went back to research and teaching at Syracuse University in 1994, we revived the book idea. We circulated our old outline, revised it, and assigned chapters. The chapters were completed in December 2001. The project took more than a decade to complete, but it now reflects our more mature understanding of social science theory structure. It was not an easy book to write, but it is some of the most satisfying work we have done.

We would like to acknowledge the influence of Jerald Hage, now in the Department of Sociology at the University of Maryland, and thank him for being a pioneer in this new and important area. We hope readers of this book will come to share our excitement about theory building and use the ideas and principles contained in this book to conduct better research and build better theories.

— Pamela Shoemaker
— James W. Tankard, Jr.
— Dominic L. Lasorsa
June 2003

Foreword

Periodic cycles apply to topics in the social sciences as they do in fashion. In the 1960s, there was considerable interest in the building of social science theory when the accent was on the word *science*. A proliferation of books on the logic of theory or techniques for theory construction was its direct manifestation. Then, in a very short time, by the 1970s, the focus had shifted to the opposite extreme, namely a distrust of theory and even an ideological opposition to the word *science*. The word *social*, as in *social construction*, has now become operative.

So when I received an e-mail from Jim Tankard that the book *How to Build Social Science Theories* (hereafter *HBSST*) was about to be published, I was excited and for several reasons. First, I had been thinking of returning to the topic of theory construction myself. Now, the publication of this excellent book frees me to move on to some of my other concerns. Here is a book in which the most important ideas in my own effort have been retained, elaborated, and improved upon in a number of interesting ways. Second, and more critically, *HBSST* is a hopeful sign of a renewed interest in building social science theories and in science as a way to make this world a better world to live, a *raison d'être* that postmodernists have failed to appreciate.

After receiving a copy of the manuscript and reading the preface, I must also admit that I was deeply touched. I had had a very strong commitment to teaching theory construction because I had always believed that many more individuals could be creative if they were provided with the right language and the right tools. This was the objective of *Techniques and Problems of Theory Construction* (hereafter *TPTC*): to deconstruct the problem of constructing good, solid, and valid theory that would withstand empirical tests into a series of manageable steps such as finding continuous variables and specifying their definitions and linkages. So I rejoiced when I discovered that Shoemaker, Tankard, and Lasorsa had had these same concerns for a number of years.

As I have suggested above, *HBSST* has improved upon my effort by

1. Providing a number of examples and in enough detail so that readers can more easily grasp quite difficult and abstract ideas involved in such notions as continuous variables, theoretical definitions, and operational linkages

2. Integrating the discussion of theoretical and operational linkages with statistics and research methodology more generally

3. Adding three- and four-variable sets of hypotheses and linkages

4. Including a whole chapter on models and their use in theory building, which can be a wonderful source of new ideas about variables

Each of these kinds of elaborations requires a few comments.

My original effort included too many new terms for the typical graduate student. Shoemaker, Tankard, and Lasorsa have rightly concentrated on the analytical importance of continuous versus categorical concepts, theoretical and operational definitions, and theoretical and operational linkages. These are the core ideas, which they have carefully explained with numerous examples. The richness of the examples, I am sure, will make these abstract ideas concrete enough so that they are comprehensible. Indeed, it is clear from the preface that the authors have spent some time teaching these ideas and learning how best to communicate them to their students.

A truly important contribution is the integration of the theoretical ideas of operational definitions and linkages with statistics. In particular, Chapter 4 has a rich variety of examples that make apparent the connection between theory and research. I do not know if graduate departments of mass communication resemble those in sociology, but I do know that in the latter there has been a wide separation between those interested in theory and those interested in research. This chapter, like other parts of the book, narrows the distance between these alternative ways of thinking.

At the time I was writing *TPTC* (in 1968, while I was living in Birmingham, England, and teaching at the University of Aston), path analysis did not exist, and it was difficult to get students to think in terms of independent and dependent variables, let alone anything more complex than this. But today three- and four-variable analyses are commonplace. *HBSST* has a separate chapter devoted to each of these issues, which is wise indeed. The three-variable case is a paradigm that is well integrated with the analytical strategies of Columbia University (taught by Paul Lazarsfeld and Herbert Hyman, by whom I was trained as a graduate student) and is another illustration of how theory and research can be usefully combined. The next chapter examines the set of concerns involved in analyses of four and more variables.

What could also be added to the latter discussion is the importance of combining alternative paradigms as a fruitful theoretical and research strategy. Sociology, like many of the social sciences, has been riddled with controversies over the past few decades. It seems to me that rather than debating opposing viewpoints it is much more fruitful and appropriate to include them within the same research study. Of course, one might question whether it is possible to represent another perspective accurately when one is committed to a specific viewpoint. Each of us has to provide his or her own answer to that question. But without a doubt, the field advances more assuredly when opposing paradigms are combined in the same theoretical framework and data analysis.

A special chapter on the use of models constitutes a wonderful addition to the armamentarium of theoretical thinking. Indeed, models can be a useful source for generating hypotheses or theoretical linkages. Again, ideally, one would like to combine several of them relative to a single subject.

Now, who does this book address? All its examples involve the field of mass communications, yet the book is entitled *How to Build Social Science Theories.* Though it would seem to have a very specific audience in mind, I would argue that it should be read by anyone preparing for a career in social science research, whether in an academic, governmental, or private sector setting. Researchers—and this necessarily includes PhD candidates—are required to frame their subject matter theoretically, indicating what is missing and suggesting what might be helpful in filling the gaps in knowledge. The separate chapters as well as the discussion of evaluation provide a framework to do just that—determine the missing parts—and provide ideas about how to eliminate knowledge gaps. Increasingly, people hired with either MSs or PhDs are asked to demonstrate that they have this capacity to generate new theoretical concepts and hypotheses. Certainly, this is the gist of questions I have been asked to answer when writing references for students who have used my name. This book can help them in this endeavor and ensure a more successful career for them.

Finally, and because the last chapter touches on the problem of creativity, let me make a few comments about this issue. Without the same labels, many of these ideas were buried in the examples in my own book *TPTC* in specific discussions of how to think about a new concept, operational definition, or theoretical linkage. Creativity in thinking is also affected by the variety and sources of information that we monitor, as any student of mass communication would probably agree with. Here are some the ways in which the variety can be increased:

1. Cultivating a diverse set of friends in terms of age as well as culture, politics, and religion

2. Knowing multiple languages well enough to be able think in them

3. Living in another country and adapting successfully to its culture rather than remaining in an American ghetto

4. Reading books and newspapers or listening to television or radio programs, especially when foreign, that disagree with our cherished perspectives and attempting to understand their criticisms of our own ways

5. Taking double majors in college or shifting disciplines between college and graduate school, especially if they represent disparate ways of thinking

6. Studying and working in teams, learning how to read the other team members' feelings and hidden ideas

The list could be extended, but one can easily see that the general theme is learning how to live with diversity, embracing it and understanding it. This leads to much more complex cognitive structure, which in turn will facilitate creativity in our own minds and lead to our developing new continuous variables, theoretical and operational definitions, and theoretical and operational linkages.

Let me close by saying once again how delighted I am that so much careful thought has been given to how to communicate with students so that they can grasp the importance of thinking theoretically.

— Jerald Hage
Arrigas, France
June 2002

1

Introduction

The Nature of Science

The primary goal of this book is to demonstrate how to build theory in the social sciences. Specifically, it deals with science, social science, social science theory, and social science theory building.

❖ SCIENCE

When we say that this book deals with *science*, we greatly constrain what it is about. Although we often focus on what we know, this book is not so much about what science has taught us as about how to do science. As such, it deals not so much with what we know as with how we know. The word *science* is based on the Latin verb *scire*, which means "to know." It comes from the present participle of that verb, *sciens*, and thus literally means "knowing" (*Webster's New World Dictionary*, 1962). Science is a way of knowing. Science, however, is a particular way of knowing different from other ways of knowing, such as authority, intuition, or tenacity.

People often tell us what they know, either because we ask them or because they tell us anyway. When we ask people how they know something—why they believe it—their answer often reveals the ways of knowing they have relied upon to reach that knowledge. Some people believe that science is at odds with other ways of knowing, to the point where if one accepts science one must reject other ways of knowing. However, science and other ways of knowing are not totally incompatible. Actually, they often lead to the same conclusions, and other ways of knowing can be no less efficient and satisfying than science. If they were not, we would stop relying on them.

Relying on trusted authority, for example, can be a reasonable way to know. If my mother tells me that I should not eat too much candy because it will rot my teeth, then I may find it much more efficient and helpful to take her word for it than to attempt to question her authority and to use other ways of knowing to determine the correctness of her position.

Likewise, I may not know at all what science has to say about the value of having a household pet, and I may not care at all that my best friends strongly believe that pets are more trouble than they are worth. My intuition may tell me that my dog helps relieve stress in my life, and that may be all I need to know about it.

We sometimes hold something to be true simply because it has been that way for as long as we can remember. I have always been happy to receive paper money. I understand that it is just a piece of paper, but I also understand that it is "backed" by the government, which has reserves of gold in Fort Knox, or something like that. I do not really know all the details. In fact, when I start to think about it, I realize that my understanding is quite vague. However, paper money has always worked for me, so I am content to continue using it. We often hold on tenaciously to those things that have worked for us, as long as they continue to work.

In many cases, nonscientific ways of knowing such as authority, intuition, and tenacity serve us well. Much of what we know about ways of knowing comes from a wonderful book by Morris Cohen and Ernest Nagel, published in 1934, in which they explore at length the differences between science and other ways of knowing. The book is divided into two parts. The first part teaches how logic works. There we learn about syllogisms and other principles of logic. The second part teaches how science works. There we learn about hypotheses and other principles of science. It is at the beginning of this second part that

Cohen and Nagel describe so well how science differs from other ways of knowing. They make the compelling argument that science is nothing more than applied logic. Thus, they teach the principles of logic in the first half of their book, and then in the second half they show how these principles can be applied.

The major difference between science and other ways of knowing is that science applies logic to question itself constantly. We will have more to say about this later, but the point here is that this book is about one particular way of knowing, called science, and it is not about other ways of knowing, regardless of how valuable they may be.

❖ SOCIAL SCIENCE

When we say that this book applies to *social* science, we further constrain what it is about. Much of science deals with knowledge of nature and the natural world. It focuses on the study of naturally occurring phenomena and how they relate to each other, the structure of the universe, and the activity of its elements. This has become known as *natural science*. Natural science has been divided further into a number of subareas, including botany, chemistry, geology, physics, and zoology, with each of these fields concentrating on a different aspect of the natural world.

Social science, on the other hand, deals with knowledge of society and the social world. It focuses on the study of socially constructed phenomena and how they relate to each other, the structure of society, and the activity of its members. It also has been divided further into a number of subareas, including anthropology, communication, economics, history, political science, psychology, and sociology, with each of these fields concentrating on a different aspect of the social world.

There is nothing magical or mysterious about these demarcations. They are mostly a matter of convenience. Likewise, each of the subareas of the natural and social sciences is divided into further areas of specialization. One's study of chemistry, for example, may be limited to inorganic chemistry, or one's study of psychology may be limited to cognitive psychology.

When we say that this book is about the social sciences, as opposed to the natural sciences, we are not saying that the scientific method is substantially different in these two major branches of science. The natural and social sciences differ in how long they have existed, in the varieties of research methods they tend to use, and in other ways, but if one studies the scientific method in the natural sciences one will learn essentially the same general approaches to knowing as one learns from the study of the scientific method in the social sciences. The scientific way of knowing how chemical elements interact is similar to the scientific way of knowing how members of a social group interact. What differs most is the object of study. Therefore, those interested in the natural sciences could use this book to learn how to build theory in the natural sciences. What they will not find here are many particular references to and examples from the natural sciences.

Some scholars will hold that we are not going far enough here in noting the significant differences between the natural and social sciences. The eminent sociologist Robert Merton (1957) wrote thoughtfully about differences between the "more mature" sciences and the "immature" and "fledgling" discipline of sociology, noting that "between sociology and these other sciences is a difference of centuries of cumulating scientific research" (p. 87). Two major developments have occurred since Merton wrote this in the 1950s. First, sociology and other social sciences have grown. The "more mature" sciences always will have—by definition—an advantage of centuries more of cumulative scientific research, but the social sciences since the 1950s have made considerable strides in research and theory. They will always be less "mature" than the natural sciences, but as time passes these differences become less characteristic and meaningful, just as the differences between a 17-year-old human and a 27-year-old seem more substantial than the differences between a 50-year-old and a 60-year-old. Second, rather than simply adding to the cumulative firmament, some recent research in the natural sciences is calling into question fundamental beliefs about the nature of things. Previously unshakable principles, some so basic that they were elevated to the status of natural "laws," are now being challenged. A half-century ago, it was commonplace to believe that the natural sciences had a decided advantage in that their objects of study were much more predictable than those of the social sciences. If one knew the laws of motion, one could predict how a billiard ball would react when struck by another ball. A chemist could predict with great confidence how a mixture of two elements would react. The social sciences, in contrast, deal with people—objects that appear to be much less predictable than billiard balls and chemicals.

This difference was believed to be so significant that the natural sciences became known as "hard" science and the social sciences as "soft." Now these differences are not so clear, and challenges believed to be limited to the social sciences are being faced in the natural sciences as well. We now know that when subatomic particles are observed, they move in unpredictable directions. It is interesting to learn that the behaviors of people are no less predictable than the subatomic particles of which they are made. In view of these developments, we prefer to focus more on the similarities between the natural and social sciences than on their differences. We appreciate Merton's (1957) recommendation that in discussing sociological theory

> [e]very effort should be made to avoid dwelling upon illustrations drawn from the "more mature" sciences—such as physics and biology—not because these do not exhibit the logical problems involved but because their very maturity permits these disciplines to deal fruitfully with abstractions of a high order to a degree which, it is submitted, is not yet the case with sociology. (pp. 85-86)

We follow Merton's advice here and use illustrations drawn from the social sciences rather than the natural sciences, but not because we believe it is unrealistic in the social sciences to deal with abstractions of a high order. To us, it is more a matter of efficiency. All sciences, natural and social, are becoming more specialized. As research accumulates and literatures grow, it is becoming increasingly difficult to master even subareas of a discipline. We limit our illustrations here to the social sciences for two reasons: one, to help readers by using examples they may find familiar and, two, to introduce readers to new territory in related but not exceedingly distant fields.

❖ THEORY

When we say that this book deals with social science *theory*, we further constrain what it is about. The word *theory* sends a glaze over the eyes of most people. This is somewhat ironic because the word *theory* comes from the Greek *theoria*, which means "a looking at." To most people, however, *theory* seems to mean "removed from reality." Most people may not know much of anything about theory, but they see it as impractical, irrelevant, and nonessential. To them, theories are either so esoteric and complicated as to be incomprehensible or so commonplace and obvious as to be platitudinous. Either way, to most people, theories seem to be of little use.

Most people, however, misunderstand what a theory is and what a theory does. In reality, people use theories every day. They have informal theories about how to choose a bait, a date, a mate. A theory is simply one's understanding of how something works. Theories we accept we may affectionately refer to as common knowledge or common sense, aphorisms or maxims. Theories we disfavor we may disparagingly call folktales or folklore, superstitions or old wives' tales. Informal theories are handed down to us from many different sources, including relatives, friends, business associates, teachers, spiritual leaders, and government officials. As long as they work well, we tend not to question them.

Science is another source of theories. In fact, science is all about theory. The goal of science is to produce and test theories. As we pointed out earlier, the major difference between science and other ways of knowing is that science constantly questions itself. Science tries explicitly to state its theories, to pose them in formal ways using precise statements so that it is clear what they are saying, to test them, and to confirm, modify, or discard them. Science is the ongoing business of coming up with new ideas and finding ways to challenge them. This notion of testing and revising is what separates scientific theories from the informality that characterizes informal theories.

Some scientists would sneer at the idea of predicting the future, but that is precisely what they often are trying to do. The reason we want to understand how something works is to enable us to make plans, to have expectations about how something will behave, to control things better—to predict the future. Though it is true that some science is intent on explaining past behavior, with no regard for whether that behavior currently exists or may exist tomorrow, most science is concerned with explaining what is happening now and is likely to happen again. Furthermore, even the study of the past is often fueled by an interest in what it might tell us about the present and the future. Thus, although textbooks often state that theory is meant to describe, explain, or predict, theory almost always is meant to explain in order to predict. The goal of theory is not so much to explain things as to use explanations to predict things.

When science is successful, it changes our understandings of how things work. There is an irony here. Humans generally want things to be predictable. They want their planes to arrive on time, their jobs to be there in the morning, their peach trees to produce sweet peaches. The very reason humans value science is its awesome ability to allow them to predict things. How does science accomplish this goal of making things predictable? It strives to challenge and change our predictions. Science is thus a never-ending battle between the world as we think we know it and the world as we *will* think we know it.

It is also somewhat ironic that humans can be so amused at the misunderstandings of those living in the past without recognizing the extent to which they themselves are also misunderstanding things. The Earth is flat. The atom is indivisible. The speed of light is insurmountable. We believe things today that our children will not believe tomorrow. Not long ago, a daily newspaper ran a story with this headline: "The speed of light is exceeded in lab" (Suplee, 2000, p. A1). The lead paragraph said that the scientists caused "a light pulse to travel at many times the speed of light." An inset quote from one of the researchers said, "Our experiment does show that the generally held misconception that 'nothing can move faster than the speed of light' is wrong." What other "laws" of nature will become "misconceptions" tomorrow? Science is not for the faint-hearted.

❖ SCIENTIFIC JARGON

Many people get confused by the jargon used by scientists to describe what they do, and they are particularly confused by such terms as *theory, hypothesis,* and *law.* To some extent, the confusion is understandable because the differences among these terms are blurred. The differences rest on the nature of the evidence that supports the law, theory, or hypothesis. Although we have just said that we intend here to use examples mostly from the social sciences rather than from the natural sciences, in the following discussion our examples come from the natural sciences because we want to use examples with which most people are familiar, without having to explain them. Also, one would be hard pressed to find an example of a scientific law from the social sciences.

Scientists rarely elevate a scientific statement to the status of *law* because that implies that observations have been made with unvarying uniformity. Thus, scientists refer to "the law of the conservation of energy" because this is a principle of science that has never been successfully challenged. As we noted earlier, however, recent scientific discoveries are challenging even some of the most long-standing and cherished of scientific principles. Because science is in the business of constantly questioning its findings, it would seem wise to limit greatly the use of the term *law*. Perhaps science should outlaw the use of the term *law*. Some would argue, however, that the term does serve a useful purpose in that it distinguishes the many "mere" theories from the very few that have never been successfully challenged. Perhaps these do deserve a special designation to note their rare and special status.

In contrast to a scientific *law*, a scientific *theory* is a statement of science that implies considerable evidence but not complete uniformity of findings. Given the nature of science, it is therefore understandable why science consists primarily of theories and research testing theories. Because theory implies the existence of competing ideas, theories are by nature controversial. Scientists also may disagree about what constitutes "considerable" evidence. The scientific method is designed to help scientists resolve such debates, but the fact remains that scientists are humans and humans make mistakes, so there is always a certain amount of fuzziness and uneasiness surrounding theories. If scientists can be wrong about scientific laws, they certainly can be wrong about scientific theories. Thus, although there is a vast amount of evidence supporting the theories of electromagnetism, evolution, and relativity, it is perhaps better to think of them nonetheless as theories rather than as laws.

Considerably more confusion exists regarding the differences between a *theory* and a *hypothesis*. Even dictionaries can lead one astray. *Webster's New World Dictionary* (1962), for example, defines a hypothesis as an "unproved theory." However, no theory is ever completely proven or disproved (Popper, 1968)—that's what makes it a theory and not a law. The sort of thinking that treats a hypothesis as an "unproved theory" contributes to the confusion of these terms. Thus, Webster's defines the nebular hypothesis as "the theory that the solar system was once a nebula which condensed to form the sun and the planets" (p. 980). In actuality, the reason the nebular hypothesis is a hypothesis and not a theory is that it lacks enough evidence to support it. If and when enough compelling evidence is gathered, the nebular hypothesis may be raised to the status of a theory. A hypothesis is a scientific statement that asks to be tested. Thus, new scientific ideas are by definition hypothetical. With considerable evidence, they may become scientific theories. If they ever reach the point where every observation invariably supports them, they may even come to be called scientific laws.

❖ DOING SCIENCE

Science has contributed much to our understanding of how the world works, and many books have been written describing the discoveries of science. New students of psychology, chemistry, anthropology, economics, and other sciences will read about the major theories in the history of their discipline, the research that has been done to test those theories, and the leading contemporary theories and research. If they are successful, these students will take this knowledge and apply it, becoming practitioners in their field.

Some of these students, having learned what science is, will endeavor to do science. They will turn to a smaller set of books, those that teach the student the methods of science in their field. They will read about how to conduct research in order to test theories and to improve methods. If they are successful, these students will take this knowledge and apply it, becoming researchers in their field.

Some of these students, having learned what science is and how to do it, will endeavor to change science. They will turn to an even smaller set of books, those that teach the student how to create theories in their field. They will read about how to build new models of things that offer better understandings of how they work. If they are successful, these students will take this knowledge and apply it, becoming theory builders in their field.

It is for these last few students that this book is written. Our hope, however, is that this book will increase the numbers of those interested in doing this most difficult job of science—creating new theories.

The authors of this book remember well their advanced formal studies that included readings about theory building. Because we all now regularly teach advanced theory and methods courses, we also get to relive with our students the experience of being introduced to this difficult topic. There is just no getting around it: Building theory is a tough job, and learning how to build theory is almost as challenging.

Theory building is difficult because it requires both great discipline and great creativity, and although a person may possess one of these attributes, few people seem to possess both. In fact, we suspect that those who possess one of these attributes are likely not to possess the other—that those characteristics that make for a great disciplinarian do not make for great creativity, and vice versa. But that is just an untested hypothesis we have. What we do know, tried and tested from many personal experiences, is that theory building requires excruciating attention to detail coupled with wild flights of imagination. About the only solace we can give those about to embark on theory building is that it probably won't kill you and that if it doesn't kill you it probably will make you stronger.

Theory building requires hard work, but, unfortunately, hard work isn't enough. Theory building also requires an ability to see things that others have not been able to see, to synthesize disaggregated parts into a new whole. It is this part of theory building that is perhaps most frustrating. For though it is possible to teach someone to work hard, how do you teach someone to be creative?

The eminent social scientist and teacher William McGuire (1976) grappled with this question. He claimed that social science instruction devotes at least 90 percent of its time to teaching students ways of testing hypotheses and that "little time is spent on the prior and more important process of how one creates these hypotheses in the first place" (p. 40). This neglect of the creative phase of science, he argued, probably comes neither from a failure to recognize its importance nor from a belief that it is trivially simple; "rather, the neglect is probably due to the suspicion that so complex a creative process . . . is something that cannot be taught" (p. 40). But although he admitted that "creative hypothesis formation cannot be reduced to teachable rules" and that "there are individual differences among us in ultimate capacity for creative hypothesis generation," he nevertheless maintained that "we have to give increased time in our own thinking and teaching . . . to the hypothesis-generating phase of research, even at the expense of reducing the time spent discussing hypothesis testing" (p. 40).

We agree with McGuire that social science would benefit greatly if we devoted more attention to teaching future scientists to be both creative and critical in their approach to their work. It is in this spirit that we write this book. That is the task we have set before us, and it is no easier a task than the one we ask the reader to assume.

❖ OUTLINE OF THE BOOK

In this chapter, we have attempted to make it clear to the reader what this book is about. In the process, we briefly noted some of the essential ideas, such as what a theory is and why we need theory. These ideas will be explored more fully throughout the rest of the book.

Theory building is a process that can be broken down into a series of steps. We have designed the book so that each of the subsequent chapters covers one of these steps. Although it is possible to read the chapters out of order and to read any one chapter independently of the others, the best way to understand fully the process of constructing a theory in the social sciences is to master each chapter in turn. We feel confident that the patient and careful reader who follows this plan will be rewarded.

Let us focus for a moment on the importance of patience. One of the great obstacles to learning how to build theory is the jungle of jargon one encounters whenever exploring this subject. Students can quickly become frustrated when faced with myriad terms that are sometimes distinguished without appearing to have any meaningful differences and at other times are used interchangeably when meaningful differences exist. We have already encountered disputes about the "proper" use of terms such as *law, theory,* and *hypothesis.* One of our primary goals in writing this book is to attempt to bring some order to this bewildering and confusing use of jargon. This requires both discipline and patience on the part of the reader. In each chapter, we introduce an important step in theory building, we identify the important elements of that step, we define these elements, and we note how they are similar to and different from other terms found in the literature of theory building. Thus, when we introduce the idea of *concepts,* we note how they are similar to and different from other ideas, such as *constructs.* We then state when and how we will use important terms, which terms we will ignore, and why. Then, when we move on to the next step in theory building, we use only the selected terms.

The rest of this chapter describes the remainder of the book. We hope that the reader will give each chapter the attention it deserves before moving on to the next. In this way, the reader will learn the challenging activity of theory building with the minimum amount of difficulty.

Chapter 2 introduces the concept of concepts. As the chapter title notes, we consider theoretical concepts to be the building blocks of theory. Theories are statements, and statements are made up of concepts. Our first job in theory building, then, is to identify and define the concepts in our theory. Chapter 2 discusses the various types of concepts used in theories, as well as distinguishing concepts from other terms used in theory building. In this chapter we will learn about the differences between concepts, constructs, and variables and why these differences are important in building theory. We then will discuss the notions of independent versus dependent variables, categorical versus continuous variables, and dimensions, which are ways of converting categories into continua. We also will explore the differences between theoretical and operational definitions and the "meaning space" of a concept. At least some of these ideas probably sound unfamiliar to you, but once you are able to identify these basic elements of theory building, you will be ready to consider how to use them to construct your own theory.

Beginning with Chapter 3, we discuss ways to combine concepts into theoretical statements. We start with the simplest case, which is the construction of a theoretical statement relating just two variables. Just as there is an array of terms similar to *theoretical concept*, there is an array of terms similar to *theoretical statement*. We will identify the commonly used synonyms and related terms, including *axiom, postulate, hypothesis, assumption, theorem,* and *proposition,* and show how they are alike and different. We also will discuss the difference between a research question and a hypothesis and between categorical statements and continuous statements and why these differences are important in theory building.

In Chapter 4, we discuss theoretical and operational linkages. Once we have produced a theoretical statement, the next step in the theory-building process is to state explicitly why we think this statement makes sense. The rationale for our theoretical statement is called a *theoretical linkage.* Suppose, for example, that we suspect that the more television violence a child watches, the more aggressive the child will become. The theoretical linkage for this statement would include the various reasons supporting our hunch. These might include research that shows how children learn to model behavior they see on television and studies that demonstrate how children are attracted to violent content on television. The theoretical linkage builds our case for our theoretical statement. It is our argument for why we think it is reasonable to believe that one concept, such as television violence, may be connected to another concept, such as child aggression, in the way that we have specified.

Once we have laid out *why* we think our concepts are connected, we lay out *how* we think they are connected. This is called the *operational linkage*. Some connections between concepts may be simple, but others may be complex. For example, it might be the case that a little television violence has no discernible effect on aggression but that as viewing becomes heavier, aggression increases exponentially. Or the opposite might be true, so that just a taste of television violence might have a profound effect on aggression and additional increments have little added impact. The operational linkage describes explicitly how we think the concepts in our theoretical statement are related. In Chapter 4, we also introduce a particular and important kind of connection between concepts, the causal relationship.

In Chapter 5, we extend our discussion of theoretical statements to those containing three concepts. Here, we explore how three variables might be related, including the notions of control variables, contingent conditions, and intervening variables. Five types of three-variable relationships are identified. We also discuss how to express three-variable relationships in hypothesis form, as well as theoretical and operational linkages for three-variable relationships.

Chapter 6 continues and concludes our discussion of theoretical statements with a treatment of those that relate four or more variables. As we will see, the addition of just one variable to a theoretical statement can greatly complicate it, and strategies for dealing with this complexity are suggested.

Chapter 7 introduces the notion of theoretical models and how to use them to build theory. As we will see, a *model* is not the same as a theory, but a model can be employed as a form to represent a theory. A model simply represents an object or process so as to highlight its key components and their connections. We also will discuss how to derive theoretical statements from models.

In Chapters 2 through 7, we describe the process of theory building as a series of steps leading from the identification and definition of concepts to the expression of their relationship in a theoretical statement, the construction of a rationale, and the specification of measurements. If one knows this format for the production of a scientific theory, then one is well prepared to build theory. Generating a good theory, however, requires more than knowledge of the rules. Following these procedures, one can produce a theory that is brilliant or one that is pedantic. The subject matter of the theory, the insights it produces, the contributions it makes to the advancement of science—these will depend upon the creativity of the theory builder. In Chapter 8, we discuss ways to think creatively in order to produce an insightful theory. Some may argue that it is impossible to teach someone to be imaginative, but we beg to differ. In this chapter, we suggest some techniques and exercises for producing the creative spark that can lead to a significant theory.

In Chapter 9, we discuss the uses of theory and the criteria for evaluating a theory. Here we also promote an effective approach to research known as *strong inference,* and we cover important constraints on theory building that every theory builder should know and try to address.

2

Theoretical Concepts

The Building Blocks of Theory

C oncepts are the building blocks of theories—the things being studied, compared, and related to one another. A concept is an abstraction that describes a portion of reality. It is a general name for specific instances of the phenomenon described. For example, the concept education (a generalization) describes the aggregate of people's specific learning experiences. The concept mass media use (a generalization) describes the aggregate of individuals' specific reading, viewing, and listening behaviors with the mass media.

❖ CONSTRUCTS, CONCEPTS, AND VARIABLES

The terms *construct* and *concept* are sometimes used interchangeably, with one scholar referring to a term as a concept, and another as a construct. Differences in the use of the terms *construct* and *concept* center on assumptions about just how abstract the generalization is, with constructs being more abstract or general than concepts. For example, we could call *mass media use* a construct that includes the following more specific concepts: television exposure, newspaper exposure, radio exposure, and magazine exposure.

Then we could break these concepts down into even more specific units, which might be called *variables*. The concept *television exposure* itself incorporates many more specific ways of describing media use:

- The number of days per week spent watching television
- The number of minutes per day spent watching television
- Which types of television programs are watched
- When television is watched
- Whether shows are watched when they are originally transmitted or later on videotape or digital medium (time shifting)

The list could go on almost indefinitely, for there are many ways in which concepts (or constructs, for that matter) can be measured. It is at the point of measuring a concept or construct that the term *variable* is used. Of the terms *construct, concept,* and *variable,* the last is the most concrete and specific. A variable is a measurable version of a concept or construct that can take on two or more values. A *value* represents some part or quantity of the variable: For example, the variable *education* could take the values "did not complete high school," "high school graduate," "some college," and "college graduate."[1]

Because the terms *construct, concept,* and *variable* are often used interchangeably, the similarities between them are more important than the differences. In this book, we will use the term *variable* if we are discussing the measurement of something and *concept* for more general or abstract discussions. We will reserve the term *construct* for instances where we want to describe something that is very abstract.

Variables Versus Nonvariables

Not every concept is equally useful in theory building; concepts are valuable only to the extent that they may be related to other concepts. For a relationship between two concepts to exist, each must be a variable. A concept that is a variable can take two or more values, whereas a concept that is a *nonvariable* cannot be broken down into smaller parts.

For example, the concept *female* is an abstraction that describes a specific biological characteristic. Surgery and rare events of birth aside, a person is either female or not; there are no gradations of femaleness.

(We can talk about the variable *femininity*, of course, but that is a different concept—a variable that is socially constructed and not biologically determined. Both males and females can be described as more or less feminine.) What variable could we use instead? The variable *biological sex*, which takes the values "male" and "female," should be substituted for the concept *female*.[2]

An example shows why this is important. Perhaps we want to study women's use of magazines, and we want to see whether we can support the statement "Females read a large number of magazines each month." Although this statement contains two concepts (*female* and *magazine reading*), it cannot be called a hypothesis because only the latter is a variable. Therefore, a relationship between the two concepts cannot be established, and we are left with a statement that contains only one variable, magazine reading. Although support for such a proposition may be interesting, the fact that only one of the concepts is a variable reduces the usefulness of the statement in theory building: Propositions perform only one theoretical function—they *describe* the average value that one variable takes for a subgroup of the population, the amount of magazines females read. If we want to proceed to explanation or prediction, we need to create a testable hypothesis: for example, that females read more magazines than males do.

By substituting the concept *sex* for the concept *female*, we have replaced a nonvariable with a variable. This converts a one-variable statement into a two-variable hypothesis that is testable using statistics. One-variable statements made about one segment of the population, such as "Females read a large number of magazines each month," may hide assumptions about the relationship between population subgroups: For example, "everyone knows" that women read a lot more magazines than men do. By replacing the nonvariable with a variable, we expose the assumption and make it into a testable hypothesis.

In addition, the testable hypothesis provides a way to give meaning to the phrase "a large number." Although we can measure the number of magazines that women read, we have no objective way of saying whether this is a big or little number. By comparing women's reading to men's, we have a point of comparison and can say that women read more or fewer magazines than men.

In this specific example, however, we should also ask whether using sex as the independent variable (causal predictor) gives us much explanatory or predictive power. Categorical variables such as *sex* are often surrogates for continuous variables such as *motivation, interest, usefulness*, and so on. Variables such as these might better allow us to explain why a person's magazine reading is high or low. Do women and men read magazines because of their biological sex or because they find magazines interesting or useful?

Variables Acting as Nonvariables

Sometimes a concept that is ordinarily a variable will in a particular study act as a nonvariable: That is, nearly everyone in the sample gives the same answer to a question, or over time people's answers don't change. In these instances, the concept will not be useful in statistical tests of the hypothesis because there is no variance to be explained by another variable or no variance to be correlated with another variable.

For example, if we want to establish that the number of newspaper stories about illegal drugs is related to public opinion on drugs—the more newspapers cover illegal drugs, the more people will say drugs are the most important problem facing the country (Shoemaker, Wanta, & Leggett, 1989)—then we must show that changes in newspaper coverage and changes in public opinion occur together. If one or the other never varies (for example, public opinion is constant), then no relationship can be established. If, no matter how newspaper coverage of drugs varies, there is no change in public opinion, then we cannot establish that the two concepts are related.[3] We cannot show covariance (that two things vary or change together) when one concept is a variable and the other a nonvariable.

In the above hypothetical example, public opinion about drugs is described as a nonvariable; however, no one would argue that public opinion about drugs could never vary in other studies at other times. Public opinion seems inherently to be a variable, either between topics at one time or within the same topic over time. Though it might be a nonvariable over a specific time span or for a particular topic, it is not hard to imagine instances where public opinion does vary. Therefore, whether a concept acts like a variable or nonvariable in a particular study may be due to situational factors.

Independent Versus Dependent Variables

Theories generally are aimed at establishing causal direction, that one thing causes another and not vice versa. Another term for the presumed cause in a hypothesis is *independent variable*, whereas the presumed effect is the *dependent variable*. In other words, the dependent variable's value *depends* on the value that the independent variable takes.

In the hypothesis above—females read more magazines than do males—causal direction is obvious. Although there is no way that reading magazines can change your sex, being female or male may affect how many magazines you read. Therefore, *sex* is the independent variable, and *magazine reading* is the dependent variable: The value of the dependent variable (number of magazines read) *depends on* the value of the independent variable (whether you're female or male).

In another example, we can study why the number of pages in newspapers changes from day to day. Our hypothesis is that "the more advertising a newspaper sells for a day's issue, the more editorial content (e.g., news, opinions, features) it publishes." The hypothesis predicts that an issue with lots of advertising pages will also have lots of editorial pages, resulting in a large newspaper. If there are fewer advertising pages, there will be fewer editorial pages, and the paper will be smaller. Which is the cause and which the effect? It seems clear that the writer of the hypothesis is implying that the *number of advertising pages* is the cause (independent variable), whereas the *number of editorial pages* is the effect (dependent variable).

In other hypotheses, causal direction is not as obvious. For example, studies (e.g., Chaffee, Zhao, & Leshner, 1994; Lowden, Andersen, Dozier, & Lauzen, 1994; McLeod et al., 1996) have shown that interest in politics covaries positively with newspaper reading: The more people read a daily newspaper, the more interested they are in politics.[4] But do changes in newspaper reading cause changes in political interest, or do changes in political interest cause changes in newspaper reading? Or could both be true?

Most statistics, such as correlation and regression coefficients, do not provide direct evidence as to causal direction. Although the researcher may make assumptions about which variable is independent and which dependent, a statistically significant correlation coefficient based on data collected at one time point cannot provide support for or against this assumption. It merely indicates that the observed direction (positive or negative) and strength of the relationship between the two variables in the sample elements probably also occur in the population.

Establishing a causal relationship requires more than showing the presence of covariation: that is, that a relationship or correlation between the two variables exists. A second criterion is establishing that changes in the independent variables occurred before changes in the dependent variables. In this example, establishing time order (i.e., that changes in newspaper reading occur before changes in interest and not the reverse) is important in demonstrating which variable is independent and which dependent. Third, we must rule out alternative explanations for the observed relationship. In randomized experiments, this is done by random assignment of subjects to treatment groups. In other research methods (e.g., surveys, content analysis), it is necessary to *identify* variables that are potential alternative explanations, *operationally define* them, and use *statistical controls* to rule out variance in the dependent variable that they account for *before* looking at the covariance between independent and dependent variables. Fourth, it is necessary to *control error variance.* In statistical terms, any variance unaccounted for by the independent variables is error variance, possibly due to alternative explanations unaccounted for; however, error variance could also be due to inadequate operationalization, errors in study design, or other flaws.

Categorical Versus Continuous Variables

Just as all concepts are not equally useful in theory building (variables being more useful than nonvariables), we generally say that continuous variables are more useful than categorical variables. A *categorical* variable is one whose values represent theoretically discrete parts or amounts of the thing being studied. The values cannot be broken down any more finely. A *continuous* variable represents a theoretically unbroken whole whose parts cannot be distinguished one from the other except by arbitrarily dividing the continuum into categories.

Biological sex is a categorical variable. Its two values are "male" and "female," and neither can be broken down any more finely; there are no degrees of maleness or femaleness. In contrast, *masculinity* and *femininity* are both continuous variables: They describe socially constructed norms about the characteristics ideally associated with men and women. We can easily imagine situations where Person A is ever so slightly more masculine than Person B because the concept *masculinity* represents an unbroken theoretical whole. It can be broken down into units as numerous and small as our capacity to measure them. Although we can theorize—and theoretically define—a continuous variable as an unbroken continuum, measuring a continuum requires partitioning the theoretically unbroken whole into arbitrary units. The only constraints against our measuring smaller and smaller gradations of a continuum are time, money, and the availability of an appropriate measuring tool (for example, a ruler that measures to the nearest 100th or 1,000th of an inch instead of 1/16th of an inch). But these are very real constraints, and we often find ourselves measuring the values of a theoretically continuous variable in what actually may be rather crudely partitioned categories.

For example, *time* is clearly a continuous variable. To measure the passage of time, however, we have to create a measuring scheme: We have to select the smallest unit (or *category*) of time to be measured. We can measure time in extremely small units (such as the nanosecond, one billionth of a second) that preserve much of the spirit of the continuous variable, but it is impractical to ask people to estimate their television viewing in nanoseconds or even seconds. We would be more likely to use one of these three scales in response to the question "On the average weekday, how much time do you spend watching television?"

- Interviewer: Code for number of minutes.
- Interviewer: Code to the nearest half hour, e.g., 0, 0.5, 1.0, 1.5, to maximum of 24 hours.
- Interviewer: Code to the nearest whole hour, 0 to 24 hours per day.

Or we might even ask the respondent to pick one of the following categories:

1. None

2. A little

3. A moderate amount

4. A lot

Which measurement scheme should be used? It is clear that these examples proceed from most precise to least, from seconds to a very rough approximation of time spent. Either of the first two examples preserves more of the continuous nature of the concept than does the last one, so we probably wouldn't select the last. At first glance, measuring television viewing in minutes seems best because it is the most precise, but perhaps people think about (and can most easily report on) time spent with television in the units in which television programs are offered—hours and half hours. Selecting the most precise unit of measurement (e.g., "seconds" instead of "hours") will not necessarily give us more precise results. We must consider the accuracy with which people can self-report their television viewing in seconds, minutes, half hours, and hours. If people cannot accurately self-report their television viewing time in seconds, then the result may be less precise even though the scale is more continuous.

Regardless of the option we select, however, it is obvious that the only practical options are, at some level of precision, categories of the continuous variable. If we measure time in hours, is it still a continuous variable? Our position is that *time* is theoretically continuous and that our measurement scheme is a compromise between precision and practicality. Can we use an "hours" scale in statistical tests requiring continuous variables? Yes, because the scale is still continuous. It is best to use measurements that retain as much of the continuous nature of the scale as possible, within the constraints of practicality.

Converting Categorical Variables Into Continuous Variables

For theory building, it is best to use concepts that are continuous rather than categorical variables. Measuring theoretically continuous variables as precisely as possible increases accuracy and the amount of information acquired. Statistical tests each require a specific minimum *level of measurement* for the variables being used. Categorical variables are measured with scales that are generally at the *nominal* level of measurement. The statistics available for use with nominal variables are not as powerful as those that require continuous variables—the *ordinal, interval,* and *ratio* levels of measurement.[5]

Whenever a categorical variable seems to be the best choice for testing a hypothesis, we should always consider whether one or more continuous variables would be better. Sometimes a categorical variable may initially seem to be the best one to use in testing a hypothesis, but Hage (1972) encouraged us to ask why we are interested in the categorical variable and to consider whether continuous variables may be available that would be more useful. He suggested that theoretically continuous dimensions may underlie the categorical variables that we use. Essentially, a *dimension* is a continuous variable that represents information about the differences among the values of a categorical variable. Hage wanted us, instead of using categorical variables in our studies, to identify the underlying dimensions, find ways to measure them, and then use the dimensions as independent and dependent variables.

For example, if we are asked to develop a way to study the mass media's coverage of breaking news, our first impulse might be to use a categorical variable such as *type of news medium,* with the values "television," "newspapers," "radio," "the Internet," and "magazines." We could hypothesize that there is a relationship between the categorical variable *type of news medium* and the variable *how accurate coverage of a breaking news event is.* We then complete a study and observe that the Internet has the most mistakes, followed by television and radio, newspapers, weekly magazines, and monthly magazines. Although this is an interesting finding, we have merely described the situation; we are now left with the task of trying to explain our findings. If we ask why there should be differences between the media's response to breaking news only after our study is completed, then we have missed an opportunity to build theory. We should have asked this question before the data were collected, thus looking for underlying theoretical dimensions that would help us explain why the media may respond differently to breaking news, thus causing them to make more or fewer mistakes.

What dimensions should we consider? One might be *transmission frequency*—how often news is distributed to an audience. Which of the news media would transmit news most frequently? Here's one possible ranking of transmission speed:

1. Monthly magazine

2. Weekly newspaper or magazine

3. Newspaper with one edition per day

4. Television news (five shows per day)

5. Radio news (news break every hour)

6. 24-hour cable television headline news service (on a 30-minute cycle)

7. Internet online news service (updated every 20 minutes)

It would be possible for us to substitute this *ordinal* transmission frequency scale for the variable type of news medium, or we might even come up with a more precise way of measuring transmission frequency. For example, we could create a *ratio* scale that measured the number of transmissions per month. If the month had only 28 days, here are the values we might give the media in our study:

1. Monthly magazine

4. Weekly newspaper or magazine

28. Newspaper with one edition per day

140. Television news (five shows per day)

672. Radio news (news break every hour)

1,244. 24-hour cable television headline news service (on a 30-minute cycle)

2,116. Internet online news service (updated every 20 minutes)

This scale more accurately reflects the differences in the media's transmission schedules than does the ordinal scale because it is more precise.

What other dimensions could be used as substitutes for the categorical variable *type of news medium?* There are a large number of possibilities, such as

- Amount of news transmitted "live"
- Amount of visual information conveyed
- Complexity of content
- Time available to staff for news story preparation
- Flexibility to change plans and give late-breaking news
- Number of news stories covered

All of these could be converted into continuous measures of the variable type of news medium.

The more we know about the various media, the more likely it is that our measurement of the variable will represent the variable's theoretically continuous nature. So, by identifying several continuous variables—dimensions—that may underlie the categorical variable *type of news medium,* we create a way to get more complete information about the news media.

Identifying Dimensions of a Construct

The term *dimension* can also be used to describe groups of variables that all measure basically the same thing but in slightly different ways. For example, we might decide that there are three dimensions[6] of the construct *media use:*

Dimension 1. Amount of exposure to each of the media

Dimension 2. Types of content the audience reads/views/listens to

Dimension 3. Functions that the media fulfill

But each dimension could also be broken down into one or more variables. For example:

Dimension 1. Amount of exposure to each of the media

   Variable 1a. Days per week people use each of the media

   Variable 1b. Minutes per day people use each of the media

   Variable 1c. Number of media people read/view/listen to per day

Dimension 2. Types of content the audience reads/views/listens to

   Variable 2a. Attention to specific types of content

   Variable 2b. Frequency of exposure to specific types of content

Dimension 3. Functions that the media fulfill

   Variable 3a. Extent to which a person reads/views/listens to each of the media to get information about what's happening in the world

   Variable 3b. How successful each of the media is in fulfilling this function

In this example, we might want to reduce the number of variables—seven in all—by creating an additive index that would represent the dimensions by combining the individual variables that are a part of each dimension. This would leave us with three variables (the indexes that represent the three dimensions) instead of seven (the number of individual variables in all dimensions). We'll talk more about indexes later in this chapter.

❖ DEFINING CONCEPTS

Once we have decided which concepts to use, we must define them, both theoretically and operationally. These two ways of looking at concepts provide information about both meaning and measurement.

Theoretical Definitions

The *theoretical definition* (sometimes called the *conceptual definition*) conveys the meaning we attach to the concept and generally suggests indicators of it. We could think of the theoretical definition as the "dictionary" definition and of the indicators as "hints" about how the concept might be measured. Each concept can have a variety of meanings, so it is up to the researchers to specify which meaning they intend.

For example, the construct we used above, *media use,* can be theoretically defined as "an individual's readership, viewership, or listenership to the content of television, newspapers, magazines, radio, and the Internet, such as [indicators] exposure, content used, or functions fulfilled." Note that the end of the definition suggests some indicators of the construct, so our job isn't done: These indicators have identified three potential dimensions of media use, and we must also theoretically define each:

- *Frequency of audience exposure to media*—the extent to which an individual reads/views/listens to television, newspapers, magazines, radio, or the Internet during a specified time frame, such as [indicators] days per week, minutes per day, or the number of each that is used each day

- *Types of content the audience reads/views/listens to*—the extent to which people consume certain specified types of content (e.g., sports, news, and public affairs), such as [indicators] the amount of attention that the person pays to the specified content or the amount of such specific content that they read/view/listen to within a specified time frame

- *Functions that the media fulfill*—the extent to which people identify television, newspapers, magazines, and radio with certain gratifications (e.g., entertainment, surveillance), such as [indicators] reasons why each medium is used or the extent to which each medium gives people what they want

Multiple Indicators of a Concept

The use of multiple indicators within the theoretical definition for each concept helps us understand that each concept has a variety of meanings. In the example above, although we have suggested several indicators for each concept, these indicators can never measure *all* of the meaning implied by the theoretical definition. Hage (1972) uses the term *meaning space* to indicate the universe of indicators that a concept can take. Usually we mean more by a concept than we can measure at once. As Figure 2.1 shows, using even three indicators of a concept cannot tap all of the meaning of the concept.

Although using multiple indicators does increase the amount of the concept's meaning that is being measured, some of the indicators may be more valid than others.

Theoretical Validity of Indicators

Validity is the extent to which the indicators measure the concept we think we are measuring. We often find that we cannot use all of the indicators available in our studies and must therefore identify the ones that are most valid—that best measure the concept. Sometimes it's difficult to decide which indicators are most valid, however. How broad or specific should the concept be? How do we know which indicators are the best measures of the concept?

For example, let's say we are interested in testing the hypothesis "Watching television makes children perform less well in school." There are two major concepts: *television watching* and *academic performance*. We could define *television watching* as the extent to which a child is exposed to the content of television, such as

- Hours per day the child watches television
- Number of programs watched per day
- Preference for television viewing over reading or other activities

We could define *academic performance* as the extent to which the child does well in school or school-related work, such as

- Grades on child's most recent report card
- Teacher's other evaluation of child's academic performance
- Standardized test scores
- Amount of time per day child spends doing homework

Figure 2.1   Meaning space of a concept. A concept is never completely measured, no matter how many variables are used. In this example, the first three variables are shown to measure part of the concept, and creating a new variable (minutes/week = days/week times minutes/day) adds a bit more to measured meaning. However, the white block indicates that some meaning of the concept media use remains unmeasured. Theoretically, this is always the case.

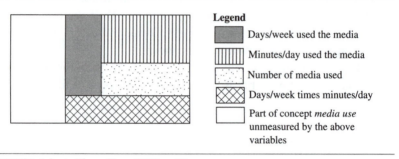

Legend

■ Days/week used the media

▥ Minutes/day used the media

▦ Number of media used

▨ Days/week times minutes/day

☐ Part of concept *media use* unmeasured by the above variables

SOURCE: Adapted from Hage (1972, p. 64).

The decision about which indicators to use will have a profound effect on the result of the study. For example, we know that the California Achievement Program's 1980 study (Comstock & Paik, 1991) used the actual hours per day spent viewing television as a measure of television watching and percentage of time doing homework as a measure of predicted academic performance. Using these two indicators *does* show that these concepts are positively related (i.e., the more television a child watches, the lower the child's academic performance). But other indicators studies using these indicators sometimes have resulted in the finding of no relationship. Faced with such contradictory findings, we would need to evaluate the validity of our indicators and perhaps do a third study with indicators we considered more valid.

Instead of the general concept *television watching*, we might want to specify our concept as *exposure to television entertainment programs*. Instead of the general concept *academic performance*, we might want to specify the *amount of time spent doing homework*. Our hypothesis would become "The more entertainment television programs a child watches, the less time the child will spend doing homework." Then we could investigate whether one or both of these variables were related to the child's academic performance.

Operational Definitions

Although the indicators in the theoretical definition hint at ways in which the concept may be measured, the full measurement scheme is specified in the *operational definition*—complete and explicit information about how the concept will be measured. This term can be confusing, because the word *definition* doesn't bring *measurement* to mind.

Whereas theoretical definitions all look much the same—like a dictionary definition—the form that operational definitions take will depend on the research method being used. Processes and procedures of variable measurement and data collection sometimes vary dramatically in various research methods because they are designed to answer different types of questions and test different types of hypotheses. We will look at examples of operational definitions for three research methods.

Operational Definitions in Survey Research

In a survey, the operational definition will probably be the text of a question and its possible responses. To measure *local television news exposure,* we might ask:

- How many days a week do you watch local television news? _____ DAYS
- On an average day, how much time do you spend watching local television news? _____ CODE IN MINUTES

Then we could multiply days by time per day to get how many minutes per week local television news is viewed.

To measure *newspaper credibility,* we might try to tap several aspects of the construct—fairness, balance, and objectivity:

- The *Gazette* is fair in its coverage of my community.

    5. Strongly agree

    4. Agree

    3. Neutral

    2. Disagree

    1. Strongly disagree

- The *Gazette* gives balanced coverage to different groups in my community.

  5. Strongly agree

  4. Agree

  3. Neutral

  2. Disagree

  1. Strongly disagree

- The *Gazette*'s coverage of my community is objective.

  5. Strongly agree

  4. Agree

  3. Neutral

  2. Disagree

  1. Strongly disagree

Each dimension of media credibility is measured using the same scale (see Babbie, 1998, pp. 141-145), and each can be considered an operational definition. It is also possible to combine the dimensions as measuring the construct *credibility*, as we will see at the end of this chapter.

Operational Definitions in Experiments

Variables in experiments are either manipulated or measured, and the type of operational definition will differ for each.

Manipulated variables in experiments are independent variables. The researcher creates an experimental treatment group for each value of the independent variable and then (in a randomized experiment) randomly assigns subjects to treatment groups. The researcher then manipulates or determines which treatment group gets each value of the independent variable. For example, we could test the hypothesis "Children who see a violent television show act more aggressively than those who see a nonviolent show." The manipulated variable would be *amount of violence*, which the hypothesis implies would have two values—violent and nonviolent. Thus, we would need two treatment groups and two television shows. If we had access to a group of children, we could flip a coin to determine which treatment group each child was in. This is a simple operational definition for the manipulated independent variable. A better operational definition would describe more about the television shows and how the level of violence was determined. The point is to completely describe how the manipulated variable is being measured.

Measured variables' operational definitions in experiments can take several forms. Sometimes a questionnaire is used to gather demographic information (e.g., sex, age, ethnicity) or to measure attitudes or knowledge. These may be independent or dependent variables, depending on the hypotheses being tested in the experiment. (Obviously, a person's sex or age is unlikely to be changed in an experiment, so these would be used as independent or control variables.) Other methods of measurement include observation, apparatuses that measure the time it takes a subject to hit a button, blood pressure, brain waves, and many more. In the example hypothesis above, we could measure the dependent variable, *aggressive behavior,* by observing children on a playground after (and perhaps before) they saw the films. We could create a list of behaviors considered aggressive, assign a coder to watch each child, and count the number of times each child exhibited each behavior. We could finish the operational definition by summing the total number of aggressive behaviors for each child, or we could further *weight* each behavior by how much aggression it represented. For example, here's how these types of aggressive behaviors might be weighted:

10. Making another child fall

9. Kicking

8. Hitting

6. Biting

4. Shoving

4. Tripping

2. Pulling hair

1. Yelling

A complete operational definition measuring aggression would have to indicate where the list and numerical measurement of aggressive behaviors came from and to demonstrate both that it was exhaustive and that the values were mutually exclusive. The operational definition would also have to specify and justify the weighting system and show how it would be applied. Generally, the number of times each behavior is exhibited would be multiplied by its weight, then the scores for each subject summed:

3 hits × weight 8 = 24 points

1 shove × weight 4 = 4 points

10 yells × weight 1 = 10 points

The total represents an aggression score of 38 points for this child, which could be compared to other children's scores. A score of 0 would indicate that no aggressive acts were observed.

Operational Definitions in Content Analysis

In content analysis studies, variables can be categorized as either content or noncontent. *Content* variables are those messages being analyzed, such as newspaper articles, television shows, films, or personal correspondence. These are often dependent variables. *Noncontent* variables are sometimes used as predictors (independent variables) of content, other times as outcomes (dependent variables). For example, Shoemaker (1984) tested the hypothesis "The more deviant journalists rate political groups, the less legitimately the groups will be covered by newspapers." *Deviance* (the noncontent, independent variable) was measured by surveying editors at the 100 largest newspapers about their attitudes toward 11 political groups. *Legitimacy* was measured with a content analysis of more than 500 articles from several newspapers. In another example, Shoemaker et al. (1989) tested an agenda-setting hypothesis: "The more the media emphasize drugs, the more people think drugs are the most important problem facing the country." They used Gallup Poll public opinion data (the percentage of people who named "drugs" as the most important problem facing the country) as the noncontent, dependent variable. The independent variable was measured by counting the number of stories about drugs in three newspapers, three television networks, and three newsmagazines.

Content variables generally have very complicated operational definitions because they have to describe the entire process of selecting the content (e.g., newspapers) to be studied: selecting the unit of analysis, the recording unit, and the context unit (Holsti, 1969) and describing the rules to be used in coding. This will almost certainly require several pages of description.

Noncontent variables may be measured by gathering data using some other research method, such as survey research, or data may be used from various archives, such as the U.S. Bureau of the Census, the Statistical Archives of the United States, or more specialized sources such as Gallup Poll data or film ratings from the Motion Picture Association of America. An increasing amount of archival data is available on the Internet or from various online subscription services such as Nexis. Noncontent operational definitions must include complete information about the other data-gathering operation or the archival data source. The goal is to provide enough information to allow someone else to replicate the study and also to ensure that the reader can evaluate the reliability and validity of the source's data-gathering methods.

Building Scales and Indexes

So far we have discussed specifying operational definitions for one variable at a time, but we have also made a case for the use of multiple indicators of a concept. In the content analysis example above by Shoemaker (1984), the concept *deviance* was initially theoretically defined with four indicators, and the concept *legitimacy* with 17 indicators. Though having multiple indicators of each concept is desirable, it would be impractical to use each indicator as a separate variable in the data analysis—the result would be 68 tests of the same hypothesis, using all possible combinations of all variables. Although it is certainly possible to do this, it seems a bit absurd. Also, interpretation of the results would be difficult if, for example, 8 of the 68 tests did not support the overall hypothesis: Could the authors conclude that the hypothesis was supported?

An alternative is to collect the data for all 21 variables but in data analysis to combine them into theoretically related concepts. Such composites are called *scales* or *indexes*, the most common of which is the result of summing the responses to two or more variables. A good scale or index will be unidimensional, have a reasonable amount of variance, and have face validity (Babbie, 1998). The terms *scale* and *index* are often used interchangeably, and these labels are even applied to operational definitions of single variables. For example, the term *Likert scale* (*strongly agree* to *strongly disagree*) is often applied both to the responses to a single variable and to composite variables in which several variables using this operational definition are added together. Conversely, Cronbach's alpha is a commonly used measurement of the reliability of an additive composite construct, which in the procedure is referred to as a *scale*. Nonetheless, in this book we will use the term *index* when we are referring to composite measures of concepts. We use the term *scale* when we are referring to the measurement (operational definition) of a single variable.

In the earlier example, Shoemaker (1984) created five indexes out of the 21 variables she used in data collection. The *deviance index* was created by summing journalists' responses to four questions measuring their attitudes toward 11 political groups. The statistical procedure factor analysis was used to look for the existence of multiple dimensions among the 17 measures of legitimacy. Four dimensions were revealed and were labeled *evaluation, legality, viability,* and *stability.* Four indexes were created by summing responses to the variables within each dimension.

The factor analysis process helps us look at whether the 21 variables are unidimensional or multidimensional: that is, whether they represent one concept in common or whether they represent several concepts that act as dimensions of an overall construct. Because one characteristic of a good index is unidimensionality, this is important information. The four dimensions that Shoemaker found suggested that the construct *legitimacy* is multidimensional. Therefore, four summative and unidimensional legitimacy indexes and the summative deviance index were created, resulting in 5 variables for data analysis instead of 21. Before summative indexes can be used, however, we must ascertain whether each index is itself unidimensional. *Cronbach's alpha* assesses the probability that each item in the index measures the same underlying concept. *Alpha* ranges from .00 to 1.00, and the higher the coefficient, the more reliable the index is. An index that is not unidimensional—that measures more than one concept—will have a low alpha.[7]

Indexes also need adequate variance and face validity. To be valid on the "face of it" means that the index's component variables *appear* as if they all are measuring the same thing. Variance can be assessed through simple data analysis that shows the distribution of values in the index and how many cases fall in each. If the vast majority of cases are clumped together on a few values, this may indicate that the index will be of limited value in hypothesis testing. An index with limited variance will not relate well to other variables, regardless of its theoretical validity. One can also look at dispersion statistics, the variance, standard deviation, and range, although these are most valuable when comparing one variable's variance with another.

❖ NOTES

1. As we will argue later, this is not a good way of measuring the variable *education* because it breaks a continuous variable into four large categories.

2. Admittedly, using biological sex as an independent variable doesn't give us much explanatory or predictive power. As we will discuss later in this chapter, categorical variables such as *gender* are often surrogates for continuous variables such as *motivation, interest, usefulness,* and so on, and these would provide more explanatory and predictive power.

3. In Shoemaker et al.'s (1989) study of public opinion and media coverage about drugs, public opinion was in fact a variable. Studies in which a concept that is assumed to be a variable turns out to be a nonvariable rarely are published. A lack of variance generally results in null findings—a lack of statistical support for the research hypothesis.

4. As we will discuss in detail in Chapter 3, the hypothetical form "The more . . . , the more . . ." implies that the first concept mentioned is the independent variable. In this case, we could just as easily have said, "The more interested people are in politics, the more they read a daily newspaper."

5. For more information on levels of measurement, see Babbie (1998, pp. 141-145).

6. In this example, each dimension is also obviously a concept; however, the term *dimension* implies that multiple concepts can be used to represent a construct. These groups of concepts can be referred to as dimensions of the construct.

7. Although we show the standard Likert scale here, it is important to remember that some people will reply *don't know* or will refuse to answer the question. These categories are routinely added to the coding scheme (although less often offered to the respondent) as 8 = *don't know* and 9 = *refuse*. Also, the assignment of the values (e.g., 1 = *strongly disagree* instead of *strongly agree*) is determined theoretically. The "most" of the concept as used in the hypothesis is generally assigned the largest valid value (e.g., 5 = *strongly agree* if the concept is agreement). The codes 8 and 9 are not considered "valid" because they do not represent *any* amount of agreement. In the case of the Likert scale, they represent types of nonresponse.

3

Theoretical Statements Relating Two Variables

W e said in the previous chapter that a *hypothesis* must be made up of at least two variables; a hypothesis expresses the relationship between two or more variables. We also referred to *assumptions* and *propositions*. In this chapter, we look at the relations between two variables more closely and distinguish among several types of theoretical statements.

Hage (1972) suggested that the term *theoretical statement* be used to describe more broadly the relationship between variables, encompassing such terms as *assumption, hypothesis, postulate, proposition, theorem,* and *axiom*. In this book, we will use three of the more specific terms—*assumption, hypothesis,* and *proposition*—with *theoretical statement* being used generally to describe all three.

A theoretical statement says something about the values of one or more variables, although it is generally thought of as expressing something about the relationship between two or more variables (e.g., "The more television a child sees, the more aggressive the child will act"). Other kinds of theoretical statements describe the values of only one variable (e.g., "There is a consistently high amount of violence on prime-time television").

We find it useful to distinguish among three types of theoretical statements:

Hypothesis—A testable statement about the relationship between two or more concepts (variables):[1] for example, "The more politically active people are, the more time they spend reading a daily newspaper." *Testable* means that social science research methodology and statistics can be applied to discover the extent of support for the statement.

Assumption—A theoretical statement that is taken for granted, not tested. The assumption may describe the relationship between variables (similar to a hypothesis, above), or it may describe the usual value of one variable in a given situation (as in propositions, below). Some assumptions may be considered untestable or may be beyond the scope of the study: for example, "The more rational the electorate, the more it is motivated to seek political information in the mass media." Others could be tested, but are taken for granted in a given study: for example, "The more politically active people are, the more motivated they are to get information about the election from the mass media." Such assumptions are often used as theoretical linkages for hypotheses: that is, reasons why the hypothesis may be supported.

Propositions are less useful than theoretical statements that address the relationship between two or more variables because they are merely descriptive and provide information about only one variable at a time: for example: "The free flow of information is valuable in a democracy." Propositions often take on a *normative* tone, in which scholars state how things *should* be, according to their ideological views.

❖ IDENTIFYING ASSUMPTIONS

Whether assumptions are propositional or relational, it is crucial for the social scientist to specify as many assumptions underlying the research and theory as possible. Assumptions are necessary (not everything can be tested) and/or convenient (pragmatism requires that not every scholar go back to the ultimate cause, e.g., the big bang). All studies are based on one or more underlying assumptions. These form the logical rationale for the study and can be used to derive the hypotheses. Although the reader does not require, for example, an assumption of evolutionary biology when reading a study of most human behavior, it is helpful for scholars to clarify their own deeply help beliefs and to acknowledge these when directly pertinent to the study. The more scholars can identify the assumptions that underlie their theories and research, the more they and others can understand the implications of the theories. If the reader does not agree with the basic assumptions underlying the research, then the rest of the work is called into question. Therefore, identifying and communicating assumptions is a form of intellectual honesty. Sometimes assumptions are not or cannot be made explicit by the researcher, and it is up to the reader to identify them.

Unfortunately, identifying and stating assumptions is one of the most difficult parts of theory building because the things we take for granted are part of our individual ideological and normative systems and are therefore transparent to our daily thought processes. Such preconscious ideas have a direct effect on the research conducted. Consider ideas such as:

- Capitalism is the best economic system.
- Men are more capable than women are.
- The unemployed lack the intelligence or motivation to find and hold jobs.
- The United States operates as a democratic political system.
- The more information people can have about political candidates the better.
- Mass media content basically mirrors reality.
- Newspapers provide more information about an election than television news programs.

Many people may agree with such statements, but establishing informal agreement is not science. Most people used to agree that the sun orbited the earth, but agreement did not make it true, and it took scientific observation to show the opposite.

Science advances by testing of hypotheses, not by assuming that certain things are true. Assumptions can be challenged on logical or philosophical grounds, but in this case one person's opinion may be as valid as another's. Social science methods and statistics provide a potentially more objective form of evaluating the relative support for a hypothesis. These methods attempt to be independent of a given scholar's personal biases and may be replicated by others. If they are replicated, we have more confidence in the original hypothesis test. Scientists recognize that no one is completely without bias and that too much bias can negatively influence the outcome of studies. Researcher bias is a threat to establishing internal validity: that is, showing that changes in the dependent variable are due to the independent variable and not to other causes.

As we indicated in the previous chapter, Hage (1972) suggested that the use of categorical variables may signal underlying assumptions that need to be specified. Why compare men's voting or newspaper reading to women's? What distinguishes men from women that makes us think that they will vote or read differently? Could there be assumptions about political interest, intelligence, and ability to understand abstract concepts, availability of time and transportation? If we can ask "why" when categorical variables are proposed, we may be able to uncover underlying assumptions, turn them into hypotheses, and actually test the extent to which assumptions are supported.

The lower the proportion of assumptions to hypotheses a theory has, the more it explains about the phenomenon at hand. Tested and supported hypotheses provide information about what the world is like. This is not the same as reaching *truth,* as Popper (1968, 1972) cautioned, but repeated hypothesis tests with consistent results do give us some reassurance about their validity. Assumptions, however, are mere guesses about the nature of the world and have no scientific support. What "everybody knows" may in fact be incorrect. Therefore, the fewer assumptions a theory contains relative to the number of hypotheses, the more power the theory has to describe, explain, and predict the world in a way than can be empirically defended.

❖ FORMS OF HYPOTHESES

Hypotheses that express the relationship between two variables can be written in a wide variety of ways, some more intelligible than others. Basically, hypotheses tell us something either about the *difference* between the average values of variables (e.g., A is on the average bigger than B) or about the *relationship* between two variables' values (e.g., as the values of A change, the values of B also change).

A hypothesis of difference could take the following form: "Canadian exports to the United States account for a greater share of

U.S. imports than the reverse." The independent variable is *country*, which has the values "Canada" and "the United States." The dependent variable is the *proportion of imports,* or, more specifically, the proportion of imports of each country that comes from the other. Such a hypothesis is testable using statistics that compare means, such as the *t* test and *F* test (analysis of variance).

Hypotheses that test relationships may take the form "if, then" or "the more, the more." For example, "If a country depends on another country for a large share of its imports, then its news media will include a lot of information about that country." This is not as useful a hypothesis form as it might seem, as we can see when we rephrase it into the more continuous form: "The more a country's imports come from another country, the more information its news media will include about the other country."

In the first form, the independent variable has two values, a "large" share and, we infer, a lesser share of imports. Likewise, the dependent variable has been dichotomized into a "lot" of information and less information. In contrast, the continuous relational form of the second hypothesis allows us to use both independent and dependent variables as continua, thus permitting the introduction into the study of countries with imports and information that vary in increments of all sizes.

It should be noted that *the form of the relational hypotheses communicates direction of the relationship.* "If A increases, then B increases" is a positive relationship because the values of the variables both change in the same direction. Likewise, "If A decreases, then B decreases" is also positive. The negative relationship, in which the variables' values change in the opposite direction, is expressed by "If A increases, then B decreases," or vice versa. The same is true of the continuous relational form: Positive relationships are expressed as "The more A, the more B" or "The less A, the less B." Negative relationships include "The more A, the less B" or "The less A, the more B." Most of the time, it is assumed that the first variable in the hypothesis, here A, is the independent variable, or cause, and the second variable is the dependent variable, or effect.

In general, we find the continuous relational form of hypotheses more useful than the categorical "If A, then B" form, for the same reasons that we preferred continuous concepts to categorical ones (see Chapter 2). As we see above, the categorical form "If A, then B" appears to provide less information than the continuous form

Figure 3.1   Both independent and dependent variables are continuous.

Hypothesis: The more education a person has, the more he or she reads a
   daily newspaper.
Operational definition for education: The number of years of formal schooling
   a person has.
Operational definition for newspaper readership: The number of days per week
   that a person inputs and processes information from a newspaper.

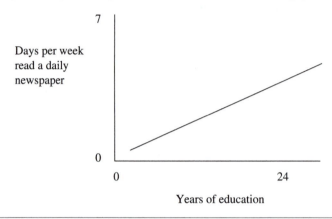

"The more A, the more B." In fact, the operationalization of the concepts in
the hypothesis defines whether the hypothesis is continuous or categorical.

Simply put, there are three combinations of categorical and continuous variables that yield three types of hypotheses:

1. *Both variables are continuous.* "The more people read a newspaper,
the more interested they are in politics." The converse could also be
supported because causal direction is ambiguous in this relationship.
The hypothesis could also be phrased: "There is a positive relationship
between political interest and newspaper reading." Figure 3.1 shows
the relationship between individuals' education and how frequently
they read a newspaper. Both variables are continuous, allowing us to
show what a hypothesized straight-line relationship would look like.
The slope of the line is arbitrary, but, as we will learn in Chapter 4, the
slope should approximate what the theory predicts.

2. *One variable is categorical and one continuous.* "Women vote more
often than men do." *Biological sex* is assumed to be the independent
variable, with number of elections voted in being dependent. This is a

Figure 3.2   The independent variable is categorical, and the dependent
variable is continuous

Hypothesis: People with a high level of education read the newspaper more
than people with a low level of education.

Operational definition for education: The distribution in Table 3.1 (number of
years of formal schooling) is dichotomized into high and low categories by
splitting the distribution at the median. (Note: This is done for purposes of
illustration only. In general, if you had a ratio-level operational definition,
you would not want to dichotomize it. You would lose a substantial
amount of information.)

Operational definition for newspaper readership: The number of days per week
that a person inputs and processes information from a newspaper.

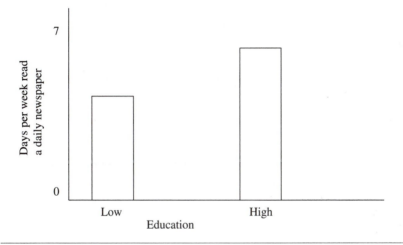

classic *t*-test statistic situation, with *sex* as the grouping variable and
voting as the variable on which means are calculated for each value of
sex. Figure 3.2 shows the same sort of relationship if we dichotomize
education. The height of the columns is arbitrary but should approximate
what the hypothesis predicts.

Although we often think of the grouping variable in a *t* test as
being the independent variable, there are also hypotheses involving
categorical and continuous variables in which causal direction is either
ambiguous or not intended: for example, "Clinton supporters are younger
than Bush supporters are." This hypothesis could certainly be tested
with a *t* test, with *candidate* as the dichotomous grouping variable and
age as the variable on which means are calculated. However, there is no
implication that changing the candidate whom a person supports will

change that person's age. Rather, the hypothesis is merely testing the difference in ages between the two groups. As always, making assumptions about causal direction is difficult and fraught with danger.

3. *Both variables are categorical:* "People with less education read the newspaper less [than people with more education]." As is often the case when dealing with categorical variables, not all values of the variables are always included in the hypothesis. Implicit is a continuation of the hypothesis: "than people with more education." Two categorical variables may easily be analyzed with a contingency (cross-tabulation) table, with the presumed cause (in this case, political party) being the column variable and the presumed effect the row variable. Making the presumed cause or independent variable the column variable is a scientific convention only, but it is one that readers have come to expect. The interpretation of a table will be based on an assumption that this format is being used. Figure 3.3 further dichotomizes newspaper reading into high and low categories, producing a 2×2 contingency table. The number of Xs is intended to be an example of the number of people who would fall in each cell, according to the hypothesis.

In the next chapter, we will discuss *operational linkages* and learn more about how these hypotheses may be represented visually. One form of the operational definition is the graph, as in Figures 3.1 to 3.3.

❖ CAUSAL DIRECTION

In the first type of hypothesis defined above, to say, "If A happens, then B will happen," implies that A is the cause and B the effect. The same is true of "The more A, the more B." The assumption is that the first variable named is independent.

In cases when it is impossible or unwise to infer causal direction, scholars may wish to substitute the form "A is [positively or negatively] related to B." This states the fact of the relationship and the direction of the relationship but does not imply causal direction. However, scholars should not use this more ambiguous relational form merely to avoid making statements that support their convictions. There are ways to argue causal direction that should be used between variables that are related. We caution scholars against using this form merely to avoid the task of establishing causal direction.

Figure 3.3   Both variables are categorical.

Hypothesis: People with less education tend to read the newspaper less [than people with more education]. (The part in brackets is implied, whether or not explicitly stated.)

Operational definition for education: The distribution in Table 3.1 (number of years of formal schooling) is dichotomized into high and low categories by splitting the distribution at the median. (Note: This is done for purposes of illustration only. In general, if you had a ratio-level operational definition, you would not want to dichotomize it. You would lose a substantial amount of information.)

Operational definition for newspaper readership: Take the distribution shown in Table 3.1 (days per week read a daily newspaper) and dichotomize it at the median. (Note: This is done for purposes of illustration only. In general, if you had a ratio-level operational definition, you would not want to dichotomize it. You would lose a substantial amount of information.)

Education

		Low	High
Newspaper reading	Low	XXXXXX XXXXXX XXXXXX	XXX
	High	XXXX XX	XXXXX \XXXXX

Causal direction may be supported in four ways:

1. The hypothesis must show statistical support for covariation (i.e., a relationship) between the two variables: As one variable changes its values, the other's values also change. Change can be in either a positive or a negative direction. In a positive relationship, the values of one variable change in the same direction as the values of the other. In a negative relationship, the values of the variables change in opposite directions.

2. The presumed cause should occur in time before the presumed effect. This is easy to establish in experiments, where the researcher has control over the timing of administering treatment variables to the subjects. In other research, such as cross-sectional surveys, however, it may be impossible to empirically establish time order, making causality more difficult to establish.

3. The researcher should rule out possible alternative explanations for the observed relationship. In an experiment, if subjects are randomly assigned to treatment groups, random assignment theoretically rules out variance due to an infinite number of unidentified and unmeasured variables. In surveys, however, researchers must use the literature to identify plausible variables that may be alternative explanations and then find ways to measure them and statistically control for them. The survey researcher's task is more difficult but not impossible. The same constraints apply to content analysis.

4. All researchers must minimize error variance. This may be as simple as ensuring that no errors are made in the study—that all subjects get the designated stimulus, that all respondents are given the same question in the same tone of voice. In practice, however, errors creep in and are inevitable in research. The researcher's job is to minimize them. Another form of minimizing error variance is controlling for important variables that are related to the dependent variable. In analysis-of-variance terms, this means keeping the error term of the equation as small as possible. The error term may include variability in the dependent variable not measured by the independent and control variables used in the study. The larger the error term, the less likely statistical significance is to be achieved.

❖ HOW RESEARCH QUESTIONS AND HYPOTHESES DIFFER

The appropriate use of hypotheses and research questions lies primarily in whether one is engaged in deductive or inductive research. The deductive model of science begins with theory, forms hypotheses, collects data to test the hypotheses, and then if necessary revises the theory. Inductive research begins with the data. It forms generalizations that become theory and may be later tested deductively. Although deductive research is ideal to test theories, inductive research is better at building theory.

Research questions are most appropriate in new areas of research in which little is known about the relationships among variables and in which there is scant literature that is applicable. Otherwise, hypotheses should be stated. With the explosion of social science research in recent decades, it is difficult to imagine a study proposal unrelated to any line of previous research. Although the topic may be new, as in the case of a new technology, there have been numerous studies about how people and society relate to new technologies, and surely these can suggest hypotheses for testing. Researchers should not avoid framing hypotheses merely because they are not sure whether they will be supported. Sometimes it is even more important to know that a hypothesis is not supported than that it is.

Research questions should be used only when there is a legitimate need for inductive theorizing. They should never be a substitute for a wide-ranging literature search and critical thinking on the part of the scholar. For example, "Does the nature of the protagonist affect how aggressive children are when they see televised violence?" is one or more hypotheses in disguise. The scholar should tap into the literature dealing with identification, fantasy versus reality of presentation, and so on, to form one or more hypotheses about this topic.

The primary danger with research questions is that the "answers" to the questions are often interpreted in the same way as hypothesis results. Yet hypotheses are interpreted narrowly. For example, in response to the question "Is there a difference between the amount that women and men read a newspaper?" it is certainly possible to observe that one mean is bigger than another. Let's say we observe that women read newspapers more frequently. The researcher confidently reports the findings and confirms that women are more frequent readers than men are. Unfortunately, the only thing established is that *in the sample* men read more than women did. But this is uninteresting information, for the purpose of most research (where less than the population is being studied) is to say something about the population, not about those individuals who by chance were included in the sample.

The same would be true if the means showed that men read newspapers more frequently. All we have established is that in this sample the means are as reported. But some researchers using research questions as confidently report one outcome as the other.

By contrast, the testing of a hypothesis requires that a direction be predicted. We look at the literature and find that in most studies men read newspapers more than women do. Thus, we frame the hypothesis "Men read newspapers more frequently than women do." Instead of using "eyeball statistics"[2] to answer the research question, we conduct a t test. The t test gives us the advantage of knowing whether the observed difference between the means is large enough to represent (at some specified probability level) a real difference between the groups in the population or whether the difference is merely due to chance or random error.

Let's say the t test does support the hypothesis and, as in the research question, we conclude that men read newspapers more than women do. Statistical significance in the t test implies that *in the population* men read newspapers more than women do, not that this is true just of the sample. This is a major advantage over the eyeball statistics used in the study with the research question.

But what if the results of the hypothesis test are different? What if the hypothesis is not supported? What if there is no difference between men's and women's reading, if women read a lot more, or if men read only slightly more? All three of these would result in lack of support for the hypothesis that men read more than women do. Does this mean that we can conclude that women read more than men do? Definitely not. The logic behind hypothesis tests requires that only statistically significant results *in the direction of the hypothesis* may be taken as supporting the hypothesis. All other results are ambiguous. Did we make a mistake in the study? Was the literature wrong? Further research may be necessary. Null results from a hypothesis test do not necessarily mean that the underlying theory is incorrect; there are many ways in which error may creep into studies, and to give the theory a fair test, the researcher must reconduct the study using different methods.

One last word about research questions: The scholar who poses research questions and then uses inferential statistics (such as the t test) to answer them is committing an error of logic. Inferential statistics are for testing hypotheses, and the researcher should reformulate the research questions as hypotheses.

❖ NOTES

1. Statistics books distinguish between *null* and *research* hypotheses. The null hypothesis is a statement of no difference between the values of a variable or no relationship between variables. Technically, the null hypothesis is tested by statistics. The research hypothesis states the

opposite, but it is generally reported in research accounts. Statistical significance implies that the null hypothesis may be rejected and that there is a certain probability that the predictions of the research hypothesis can be generalized from the sample to the population. In this book, the term *hypothesis* can be assumed to mean the research hypothesis.

2. We use the term *eyeball statistics* to indicate instances where a researcher looks at, for example, the difference between two means and says, "Well, it looks like Mean A is bigger than Mean B." But how big is big? How big a difference is enough to say something meaningful? Inferential statistics are always better than eyeball statistics, even if the two yield the same result. Inferential statistics allow us to estimate the probability of our being wrong when we say the two means are different. Eyeball statistics rely on a wing and a prayer.

4

Theoretical and Operational Linkages

Once hypotheses are formed, it is necessary to specify two sorts of linkages, connections among the variables in the hypothesis. There are two ways of thinking about such connections: First, we demonstrate why each hypothesis or research question ought to be true—that is, why the concepts ought to be related in the way the hypothesis says they are. This is the theoretical linkage. Second, we show how the concepts are related empirically. This is the operational linkage. Both are necessary if the theory is to be fully elaborated.

Theoretical and operational linkages are also necessary for propositions. The theoretical linkage explains why the proposition should be true, without concern about relations among concepts. The operational linkage shows the type of data that support the proposition.

Likewise, for research questions, theoretical linkages explain the logic of the question and justify asking it. The theoretical linkage may provide hypothesized explanations for varying (and perhaps contradictory) outcomes or answers to the question.

For assumptions, which are not empirically tested, only theoretical linkages are necessary. However, if the assumption is relational, it may be advantageous to specify some elements of the operational linkage.

❖ THEORETICAL LINKAGES

The theoretical linkage gives the theory explanatory power. It explains why the hypotheses, assumptions, and propositions should be true, using at least one of three methods. First, one can cite an existing theory and all of the explanations inherent in the theory. Second, especially if one is working in an area in which theory is not well developed, existing literature can be cited that shows results similar to (or, if one intends to refute a theory, different from) those predicted by the hypothesis. Third, and perhaps most important, researchers must be able to state support for the hypothesis in their own words using their own logic. In fact, it is desirable to state multiple reasons why, logically, the hypothesis should be true. If the researcher cannot state at least one good reason why the hypothesis is true, then the hypothesis is unlikely to receive empirical support. If the researcher can think of 10 good reasons, then the odds are greater that at least one of them will elaborate an empirically supported hypothesis. Of course, it is most desirable for the researcher to use all three methods of explaining the hypothesis under the same reasoning: existing theory, existing literature, and logical reasoning. The more evidence we can muster to support the hypothesis, the more confident we may be that it will be empirically supported.

By these methods, the explanatory power of the theory is increased. Hypotheses, research questions, and propositions are not thrown carelessly into the theory (or tested individually without thought) but are instead incorporated into a whole, showing why the concepts in the theoretical statements ought to behave in the way specified. This forces the researcher to specify ahead of statistical tests at least one good reason why the hypothesis ought to be supported. It therefore reduces the probability that the researcher will thoughtlessly create hypotheses merely for the pleasure of doing data analysis or that hypotheses will be tested only to satisfy minimal curiosity. Theoretical statements ought to be created out of a theoretical whole, and their introduction into a study is best accompanied by a strong theoretical linkage.

In fact, the group of theoretical linkages supporting the hypotheses in a study is itself the theory that the researcher presents. From what other source can it come? The existing theories, literature, and logical statements are the support for the hypotheses, and, in combination, are the theory on which the study rests. Thus, the specification of individual theoretical linkages for each theoretical statement is crucial.

In practice, most research articles are written with the literature review and theory specified in advance of the hypotheses. Unfortunately, once the hypotheses are reached, the reader may not follow the author's logic in understanding the derivation of the hypotheses, and the theoretical underpinnings of the hypotheses may not be as clear in the reader's mind as in the author's. Therefore, it is valuable to summarize the theoretical linkages given previously in one or two paragraphs, immediately following each hypothesis. This will ensure that the hypotheses are in fact directly derived from the literature and theory previously presented and that both author and reader are clear about the theoretical underpinnings of the hypotheses. Table 4.1 shows three brief examples of theoretical linkages. In practice, theoretical linkages should be more complete and elaborated upon.

The examples shown in Table 4.1 illustrate how the three types of theoretical linkage—theory, literature, and logic—can be used together to explain why the hypothesis should be supported. In areas where theory is sparse, or where the scholar is building theory, the specification of existing theory may be missing, or theories tangentially related to the topic may be mentioned. It is perfectly reasonable to build one's own logical structure to defend hypotheses; this is the creative side of scholarship that should be encouraged.

Although we have been talking about theoretical linkages for hypotheses, propositions and assumptions should also have theoretical linkages. They are especially important in assumptions, where the reader may or may not agree with the assumption after reading the justification for it.

Creating theoretical linkages for research questions presents a special case. Because no prediction is made by the research question, the theoretical linkage should not take sides—for example, present a local argument for one particular potential answer over another. However, the authors should know enough about the topic to be able to intelligently discuss the possible outcomes. Some literature may predict one outcome and other literature a different outcome. Logical arguments may be made for different outcomes. These sorts of differences should be discussed as the theoretical linkage so that we know the authors are not merely "fishing" for results but rather have thought through the research questions thoroughly and know as much as is knowable about the topic being studied.

Table 4.1 Putting the pieces together: Hypotheses from three theories

Hypothesis 1:	Concept Names:	Theoretical Definition:	Operational Definition:
The more the media emphasize an issue, the more important people think it is.	IV—Amount of media coverage DV—Importance of issue to the public	IV—Amount of media coverage is an assessment of the volume of coverage, or the degree to which a story dominates news coverage overall. DV—Importance of the issue is the degree to which the public believes that the topic is more important than other topics in the news. **Theoretical Linkage:** More coverage of an issue in the media will put it more prominently in people's minds. Over time, the focus by the mass media on an issue, such as the crime rate, will result in more people identifying that issue as an important one (McCombs & Shaw, 1972).	IV—Number of stories about crime *Range: 0 to infinity* DV—Survey responses to the question "How important is the issue of crime to you?" *Responses: 5 = very important;* *4 = important; 3 = neither important nor unimportant; 2 = unimportant;* *1 = very unimportant* **Operational Linkage:** 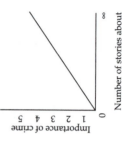

(Continued)

Table 4.1 (Continued)

Hypothesis 2:	Concept Names:	Theoretical Definition:	Operational Definition:
The more a society is integrated through shared norms, the less likely it is that its members will commit suicide.	IV—Level of social integration DV—Suicide rate	IV—Level of social integration is the degree to which the individual members of a social group feel connected to the group through shared values and a shared ideology. DV—Suicide rate is the proportion of people in social groups who take their own lives. **Theoretical Linkage:** Because suicide often is precipitated by feelings of isolation and loneliness, links to a social group through shared ideas and beliefs should reduce a person's sense of isolation. The reduced anomie at a societal level should result in a reduced suicide rate among that social group (Durkheim, 1951).	IV—The proportion of the people who are affiliated with a church or other social group (as a percentage of the total population) *Range:* 0% to 100% DV—Per capita rate of self-inflicted deaths (the rate of self-inflicted deaths per 1,000 people) *Range:* 0 to 1,000 **Operational Linkage:**

(Continued)

Table 4.1 (Continued)

Hypothesis 3:	Concept Names:	Theoretical Definition:	Operational Definition:
The greater an individual's sense of self-efficacy, the more likely it is that he or she will make a lifestyle change to improve his or her health.	IV—Sense of self-efficacy DV—Likelihood of undertaking a healthy lifestyle change	IV—Sense of self-efficacy is the degree to which someone believes that he or she can do what he or she sets out to do. DV—Likelihood of undertaking healthy lifestyle change is the degree to which someone is likely to modify a current behavior to improve his or her health. **Theoretical Linkage:** A greater sense of self-efficacy, or the ability to succeed at a task or goal, will increase the chances that a person will even attempt a behavior change. Those with low self-efficacy, and who therefore believe they are likely to fail, will see little value in even making the attempt at a healthy behavior change (Bandura, 1997).	IV—Survey responses to the question "How satisfied are you with your level of personal success?" *Responses: 5 = very satisfied; 4 = satisfied; 3 = neither satisfied nor unsatisfied; 2 = unsatisfied; 1 = very unsatisfied* DV—Survey responses to "How likely are you to start a new exercise or self-improvement program in the next 3 months?" *Responses: 5 = very likely; 4 = likely; 3 = neither likely nor unlikely; 2 = unlikely; 1 = very unlikely* **Operational Linkage:**

❖ OPERATIONAL LINKAGES

Telling how the variables in the hypothesis are related is the job of the operational linkage. Operational linkages may be presented in two forms, visual and statistical. We recommend that researchers, particularly those early in their careers, prepare both sorts of operational linkages. They will take the form of figures and statistical tables.

It is of primary importance that researchers understand that both types of operational linkages must be prepared before any data are collected. If the researchers are able to graphically illustrate what their hypotheses predict and statistically explain how the hypotheses will be tested, then they are more likely to include all variables needed to test the hypotheses. Often researchers who have not clearly thought through their studies collect and analyze their data and then wish that such and such a variable had been included. The graphic and statistical forms of operational definitions make such mistakes highly unlikely.

For beginning scholars who are unfamiliar with statistics, it is at least necessary that they prepare the graphic form of the operational linkage. This requires no knowledge of statistics and helps the researcher think through the potential testing of the hypothesis.

The graphic form of operational linkage is not included in final research projects, which place their emphasis on the degree of statistical support for the hypothesis after data analysis, not on what the hypothesis graphically predicted. On the other hand, research proposals, such as thesis or dissertation proposals, are often aided by the inclusion of graphic operational linkages because they help not only the researcher but the committee in evaluating whether all elements of the study are present and whether the student is ready to proceed with data collection.

Operational Linkages as Visual Representations

The simplest form of operational linkage is a pictorial representation of the hypothesis. For example, Figure 4.1 shows a simple graphic operational linkage for the hypothesis "The more television violence children view, the more aggressive acts they portray." The horizontal axis is generally taken as the independent variable and designated as x (see Figure 4.2), and the vertical axis is assumed to be the dependent variable, called y.

Figure 4.1   A graphic operational linkage for the hypothesis "The more
television violence children view, the more aggressive acts
they portray"

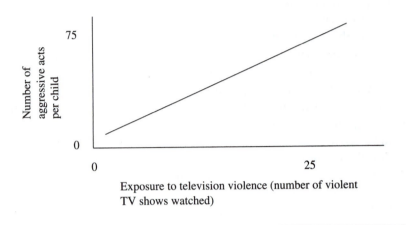

Number of aggressive acts per child

75

0

0   25

Exposure to television violence (number of violent
TV shows watched)

Figure 4.2   The *x* and *y* axes

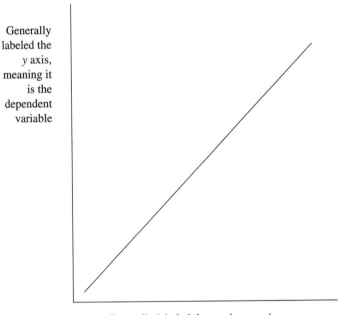

Generally
labeled the
y axis,
meaning it
is the
dependent
variable

Generally labeled the *x* axis, meaning
it is the independent variable

Figure 4.3   The data are never as neat! The line represents the closest fit
to all data points.

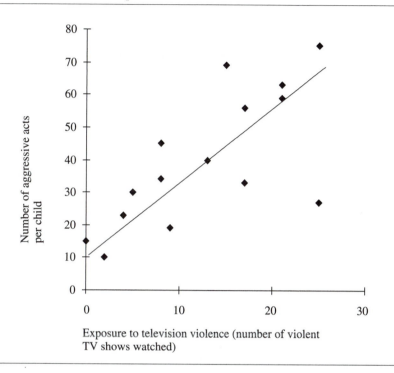

In Figure 4.3, the slanted line is a visual representation of the
hypothesis, whereas the dots represent real data collected. Remember,
we draw the operational linkage before collecting data. Once we collect
data, we will see that the reality of the data do not neatly fit the hypothesized line. The difference between our hypothesized relationship and
the data expresses how closely our hypothesis is supported.

When preparing operational linkages as visual representations, we
have four considerations: the form of the relationship (linear, curvilinear, or power), the direction in which the variables are related (positive
or negative), the coefficients (constant and slope), and the limits (the
range within which the hypothesis is supported).[1]

Form of the Relationship

As Figure 4.4 shows, relationships may be hypothesized to be linear,
straight lines. In these relationships, one or more units of change in the

Figure 4.4   Four elements of an operational linkage: the form

Linear—As the values of one variable increase, the values of the other variable
    increase (or decrease).
Curvilinear—As the values of one variable increase, the values of the other
    increase (or decrease) up (or down) to a point and then start off in the other
    direction.
Power—As the values of one variable increase, the values of the other variable
    increase (or decrease) at an accelerated rate.

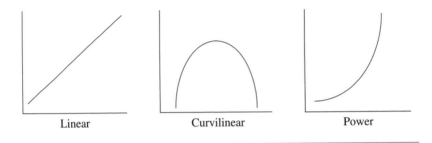

Linear   Curvilinear   Power

independent variable are accompanied by one or more units of change
in the dependent variable, in a precise and constant manner. Such
relationships are frequently hypothesized in the social sciences but
are rarely seen as pure cases. Reality rarely fits a straight line; however,
most statistics test for the presence or absence of a straight-line relationship. Thus, this basic relationship is commonly used.

Curvilinear relationships may form the letter "U" in an inverted or
upright position, or they may be shallow curves in either direction.

Power curves are a special case of curvilinear relationships, where a
change in the independent variable has a huge change in the dependent
variable at one point in the relationship. There is very little change in the
dependent variable initially, then a huge change, then very little change.

Direction of the Relationship

Here we specify whether the units of a variable change in the same
direction (positive) or in opposite directions (negative). In a positive
relationship (Figure 4.5), an independent variable's and a dependent
variable's values change in the same direction (e.g., both higher).
In a negative relationship, they change in opposite directions (e.g., the
independent variable increases in its value, whereas the values of the
dependent variable decrease in value).

Figure 4.5   Four elements of an operational linkage: the direction

Positive—As the values of one variable increase, the values of the other variable also increase.

Negative—As the values of one variable increase, the values of the other variable decrease.

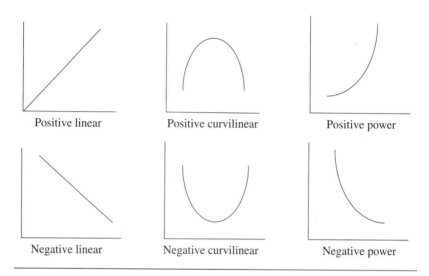

Positive linear	Positive curvilinear	Positive power
Negative linear	Negative curvilinear	Negative power

The Coefficients

The slope indicates how steep or shallow the line is (Figure 4.6). A steep line indicates that a one-unit change in the independent variable is accompanied by more than one unit change in the dependent variable. A shallow line might indicate that a one-unit change in X is accompanied by less than a whole-unit change in Y.

The constant indicates where the line crosses the *y* axis. This tells us what the value of Y is for what is generally the minimal value of X. (Exceptions occur where, for example, the scale of the independent variable ranges from negative to positive values, with zero in the center. The constant would probably be where Y crossed the zero point of X.)[2]

The Limits

As Figure 4.7 shows, increases in X may not indefinitely be accompanied by increases in Y. Take the example of the hypothesis "The more education a person has, the more he or she will read a daily newspaper."

Figure 4.6   Four elements of an operational linkage: the coefficients

Constant—The value of the dependent variable (on the y axis) when the line
    crosses the y axis.
Slope—Simply, how steep or shallow the line is. Technically, a description of
    the amount of change that we predict will occur on the y axis when the
    value on the x axis changes by 1. The larger the coefficient, the more of an
    effect X has on Y.

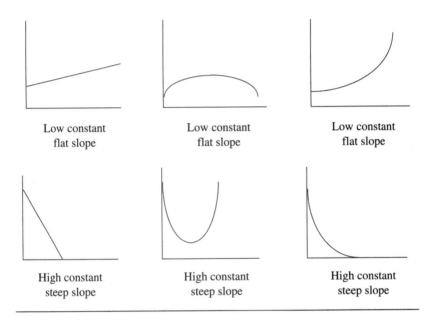

Low constant flat slope	Low constant flat slope	Low constant flat slope
High constant steep slope	High constant steep slope	High constant steep slope

A person may have indefinite years of education, but there are only 7
days a week available for newspaper reading. In reality, newspaper
reading evens off after a relatively small number of years of education,
say high school graduation or some college.

The figure shows boundary limits for linear, curvilinear, and
power relationships, but the examples illustrate only some of the
possible limits that may be hypothesized.

Operational Linkages as Statistics

Operational linkages are often expressed in statistical terms, such
as a *statistically significant and positive Pearson's correlation coefficient.*

Figure 4.7   Four elements of an operational linkage: the limits

The *limits* indicate that the relationship predicted by the hypothesis is
supported only within a certain range of its variables' values. Example:
The *ceiling effect* holds that the relationship operates only below a certain
threshold.

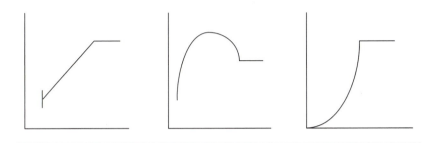

This is appropriate for the researcher to specify before the data are
collected because it keeps the researcher honest about what types of
results will support the hypothesis. In fact, it is desirable as part of the
operational linkage for the researcher to prepare tables that specify the
statistical analyses to be performed. The tables are incomplete only in
that the final numerical statistical results are not provided. Appendix A
includes examples of typical tables that may be included as operational
linkages. It is advisable to begin with univariate statistics before proceeding to inferential statistics that may begin hypothesis testing.
Bivariate and multivariate statistics complete hypothesis testing. Start
with the simple and proceed to the complex.

A major advantage of specifying in advance *all* of the tables that
will be included in the statistical analysis is that the researcher will be
sure that all variables needed in data analysis are in fact being
included. This helps the researcher in conceptualizing the study and in
ensuring that all the data needed are in fact being collected.

Appendix A does not include every table or figure that may be
needed in a study, but it covers most of the basics. To use the tables in
Appendix A, it is necessary to know the *level of measurement* of each
variable in the study. As you will see in Appendix B, levels of measurement range from nominal to ordinal, to interval or ratio. *Nominal*
variables use arbitrary numbers to represent the values of the variable.
For example, 1 can be assigned as "male" or "female" for the variable
gender. The numbers are like names assigned to the values. Nominal

variables have the characteristics of being exhaustive (all possible values/categories of the variable are represented) and mutually exclusive (an item can be placed only in one value of the variable). *Ordinal* variables include the characteristics exhaustiveness and mutual exclusivity, as well as order. That is, the numbers assigned to the values must be in a numerical and meaningful order. For example, a variable with *high, medium,* and *low* values could have them assigned as 3, 2, and 1, respectively. We cannot logically assign them as 2, 3, and 1, for the order of the numbers would not be the same as the order of the values. *Interval* variables include the characteristics of exhaustiveness, mutual exclusivity, and order, as well as having equal intervals between the numbers and their values. For example, the Celsius temperature scale assigns 100 to the boiling point of water and 0 to its freezing point. These assignments of numbers to these variables are arbitrary once order is achieved, but the scale's values are equally spaced between 0 and 100. A temperature of 80 is twice as hot as a temperature of 40. The amount of heat gained when moving from a temperature of 10 to 11 is the same as moving from 39 to 40.[3] *Ratio* variables have all of the characteristics of nominal, ordinal, and interval variables, as well as having an absolute zero. In the other three levels, zero can be assigned to any value arbitrarily. In ratio variables, zero can only mean *none of the concept.* For example, in the Kelvin temperature scale, zero represents *no heat.*

❖ THE WHOLE STORY

The specification of the operational linkage puts all of the parts of the theory together, and the theory may be shown in brief in Table 4.1. This brings together all of the parts we have been talking about in Chapters 2, 3, and 4. Although none of the three theories mentioned in Table 4.1 is complete, the table does suggest how complete theories may be elaborated. A completely elaborated theory would include all assumptions and hypotheses used, their concepts, and their definitions and linkages. This is an overwhelming task, but one that would help advance social science by making theories much more explicit than they are today and would therefore allow scholars to test the theories and advance them through support, modification, or lack of support. The current state of social science theories is much more vague, with one scholar meaning one thing by a concept and another scholar meaning something else entirely. Once definitions and linkages are specified explicitly, a base will have been established that will permit the growth of theories. Connections among theories may be made more easily, and the state of social science research will advance more quickly and with logical deliberation.

❖ NOTES

1. The following is adapted from Hage (1972), pp. 85-110.

2. The terms *constant* and *slope* are familiar to those who know regression statistics, but knowledge of this statistical procedure is not necessary to conceptually understand these terms.

3. There are occasional disagreements over what is interval and what is ordinal. For example, the Likert scale (5 = *strongly agree*, 4 = *agree*, 3 = *neutral*, 2 = *disagree*, 1 = *strongly disagree*) is treated by some social scientists as an interval scale, using the logic that values represent *equal-appearing intervals:* That is, people interpret the intervals as being equal. Others are more conservative and use this as an ordinal scale.

5

Theoretical Statements Relating Three Variables

Afrequent occurrence in communication research is to begin a line of inquiry with a hypothesis of broad, across-the-board effects, only to find in subsequent research that the effect is not general but occurs only under certain conditions. What started out as a clean, neat two-variable hypothesis needs to be qualified. The hypothesis is no longer parsimonious; it needs to have qualifying phrases tacked on. And it is no longer as general, and therefore not as potent; it holds up only in certain situations. Meadow (1985) appeared to have been referring to this occurrence when he wrote, "After four decades of exploration, we are left with one answer to the question of media effects—'it depends'" (p. 158).

Faced with this kind of outcome, we can easily imagine a process with no end. Will further research uncover still more qualifying variables, until it takes knowledge of 50 variables to make a prediction and only a computer can handle the complexity?

Meadow is right, of course, but his conclusion should not be the basis for throwing up our hands in despair. In fact, another point of view is that this is just the place at which things get interesting. As we find out more about the details of these dependencies, we are finding out something about the complexities of human behavior and the variables that make a difference. The proof of the pudding is that knowledge of the dependencies or the contingent conditions often lets us make more accurate predictions about social interactions and other forms of human behavior. In short, there's a big difference between saying, "It depends, but I don't have any idea on what" and "It depends, and the two or three most important variables it depends on are X, Y and Z."

Part of the solution to this dilemma may lie, as it often does, in taking a middle course. On the one hand, two-variable relationships are probably too simplistic. On the other hand, 50-variable relationships are probably too complicated. Even a path model with just five variables can be so complex that it is difficult to understand. But fortunately there is a range of possibilities in between these. What might make sense as a research strategy in many areas is to explore three-variable relationships, the next level of complexity beyond two-variable relationships. As we shall see, this next step increases the complexity quite a bit. And it seems like a natural step in that it takes us beyond Hage (1972), whose valuable book deals mostly with two-variable relationships.

Further, it may not be necessary to study a huge number of variables all at once. As Hirschi and Selvin (1967) noted, "The increasing success of the life sciences in understanding the human body (surely more highly integrated than the social system) suggests that good research is possible without taking everything into account at once" (p. 22).

This chapter discusses the next step in theory building in the social sciences beyond the formulation and testing of two-variable hypotheses. As Eveland (1997) noted, "Many theories . . . in mass communication and related fields predict more complex effects than the simple linear and additive effect of independent variables" (p. 405).

For instance, the knowledge gap hypothesis suggested by Tichenor, Donohue, and Olien (1970), which has generated a great deal of subsequent research, is basically a three-variable relationship. A graph illustrating the knowledge gap hypothesis is presented in Figure 5.1. The graph shows a relationship between exposure to information and knowledge, with knowledge increasing as exposure to information increases. But it also shows that the rate of increase in knowledge is different depending on the socioeconomic status of the individual. This kind of three-variable relationship is called an *interaction*. We have an interaction when the relationship between one variable and a second variable is different depending on the values of a third variable.

Figure 5.1   The knowledge gap hypothesis

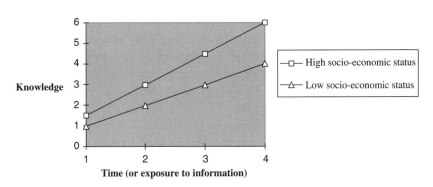

Hage's (1972) book focused on two-variable theoretical statements, for which he recommended the form "The greater the X, the greater the Y." He acknowledged the importance of relationships that are more complicated than two-variable relationships, but he didn't do very much to deal with them. He wrote:

> Through our discussion, we have been concentrating on the problem of interrelating just two variables. In practice, we can and do expect our operational linkages to be more complex than this. The diagrams and forms refer to the effect of X on some Y where X can be a combination of variables. (p. 109)

The idea that X can be a combination of variables oversimplifies the complexity of even a three-variable relationship quite a bit. As we shall see, a set of three variables can be related in five distinctive ways. The situation becomes even more complicated with more than three variables.

Of course, it is a common research strategy to introduce a third variable as a control variable while exploring a relationship. The usual reason for doing this is to test whether a relationship is spurious. This is indeed an important reason for introducing a third variable. Actually, however, there are at least three other important roles that exploring three-variable relationships can play in the development of theory.

❖ ROLES OF THREE-VARIABLE RELATIONSHIPS IN THEORY

One of these important roles is specifying the ways that a hypothesis expressing a relationship between two variables either holds up or does not hold up depending on the state of a third variable. This is sometimes spoken of as specifying the "contingent conditions" (Winter, 1981, p. 236) or as exploring "contingent causation" (Chaffee, 1977, p. 226). As Chaffee noted,

> Physically partitioning samples on the basis of contingent orienta-
> tions that are necessary for a media effect to operate is likely to
> become more common in future research; this trend is a sign both
> that we understand quite a bit about the total influence process
> and that we are going to be able to learn more. (p. 227)

An example of research that specified contingent conditions for communications effects to take place is Hill's (1985) study of agenda setting by television news. He found that agenda-setting effects are more likely when viewers have prior awareness of news topics through print media exposure or have some college education.

A second major role that exploring three-variable relationships can play in building theory is in clarifying causal relationships by showing the operation of intervening variables. This is the process of analysis that Hyman (1955) called *interpretation*. Commenting on the area of mass media effects research, Chaffee (1977) stated, "What has been lacking, although it too is beginning to accumulate, is three-variable research in which the psychological processes that intervene between media exposure and its effects are studied" (p. 222).

Chaffee (1977) gave an example of a research area where there is a need for interpretation. He cited the finding that a boy is shown a filmed fight and subsequently acts more aggressively than before. We might conclude that the film has had an effect, but we might not understand the intervening psychological process that led to this effect. In this example, there are several possible intervening processes—the boy may be imitating the behavior he has seen; the boy may be "identifying" with the grown, strong man who was fighting; or the film may have aroused him to do something physically active, and any kind of activity may have reduced that state of arousal. We don't know which of these possible interpretations is correct until we do some additional three-variable studies.

To take another example, interpretation could be useful in clarifying our understanding of how agenda setting works. We don't really know much about the process by which the play of news items in the media gets translated into a set of priorities in an individual's mind. One possibility—and this is only one of many—is that the public has a good understanding of journalism and interprets the cues of news play as indicators of importance. We could test this possibility by introducing as a third variable a new concept called *journalistic savvy*. This variable would attempt to measure understanding of the various journalism conventions used to indicate story importance. This variable could be measured by having survey respondents indicate their agreement on 5-point Likert scales with statements such as the following:

"If a news story is on the front page of a newspaper, it is important."

"The most important stories in a television newscast come at the beginning of the newscast."

"The larger the photograph that accompanies a story, the more important the story."

Once these kinds of variables have been measured in an agenda-setting study, they can be used as third variables in the kind of three-variable analysis we are recommending.

There are many other good candidates for variables that would help us understand the agenda-setting process by using a third variable to interpret the two-variable agenda-setting relationship. An excellent way to focus one's theory-building efforts is to think of possible variables of this type, figure out how to measure them, and then conduct a study in which they can be introduced as third variables along with the two principal variables of the agenda-setting process (the media's agenda and the public's agenda).

A third important reason for exploring three-variable relationships is that it can help specify the operating component of a global variable (Rosenberg, 1968). For instance, a researcher may find that whether people vote is related to social class. But *social class* is a global variable with a number of components, including education, income, social prestige, and type of occupation. Which component (or components) of social class is operating to influence voting behavior? Bringing each component variable into a three-variable analysis with social class and voting can help to pinpoint the active variable and in doing so will sharpen our understanding of the causes of voting or not voting.

❖ FIVE TYPES OF OUTCOMES

We have been focusing on a general research strategy in which two variables are cross-tabulated and then a third variable is introduced as a control or test variable. This strategy has been referred to as *elaboration* by Paul Lazarsfeld (1955a), who did much of the work to develop it. The elaboration model was first described in a paper that Lazarsfeld presented to the American Sociological Society in 1946. That paper was not published in a journal because "at that time, there was little interest in methodological discussion" (Lazarsfeld, Pasanella, & Rosenberg, 1972, p. 125). The model was first presented in published form by Patricia L. Kendall and Lazarsfeld (1950), and the original Lazarsfeld paper was finally published in 1955 (Lazarsfeld, 1955b). The strategy of elaboration research is discussed in Hyman's (1955) *Survey Design and Analysis* and Rosenberg's (1968) *Logic of Survey Analysis.*

Lazarsfeld (1955a) and Hirschi and Selvin (1967) indicated that there are four possible outcomes of this type of analysis. But there appear to be five significant ones.

In the following discussion of this kind of analysis, the terms *independent variable* and *dependent variable* will be used, even though the variables are not necessarily being manipulated in an experiment. *Independent variable* will be used to refer to the variable thought to be the causal variable. *Dependent variable* will be used to refer to the variable thought to be caused, or to be the effect. *Control variable* or *test variable* will be used to refer to the third variable brought into an expanded analysis of a two-variable relationship. An *intervening variable* is "one that is viewed as a consequence of the independent variable and a determinant of the dependent variable" (Rosenberg, 1968, p. 54).

1. *Explanation.* Explanation is one of the possible outcomes of three-variable analysis discussed by Hyman (1972). Explanation occurs when the third variable is causally prior to the independent variable and accounts for the original relationship (see Figures 5.2a, 5.2b, and 5.2c). In this situation, we conclude that the original relationship was spurious, and we discard the original relationship. This is not a total loss, however, because we have learned something about the causal relationship. We have learned that the third variable is a more plausible cause of the dependent variable than the original independent variable.

Figure 5.2a   Single people appear to eat more candy than married people
do. Is this relationship genuine, or is it spurious?

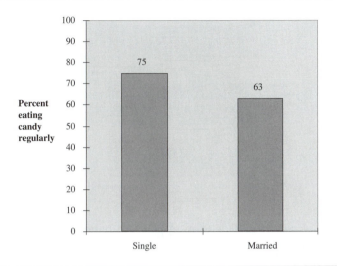

SOURCE: Adapted from Hans Zeisel (1968), *Say It With Figures*, 5th ed. New York:
Harper & Row, p. 139.

Figure 5.2b   We control for age and find that younger people eat more
candy than older people, but there is no real difference
between single and married people's candy eating. This is a
case of explanation—we have found that age is an alternative
(and better) explanation for the original relationship.

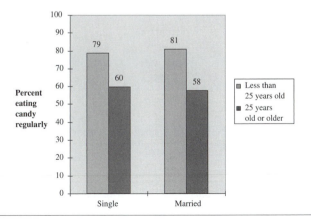

Figure 5.2c   A line graph also shows that marital status is not related to eating candy, once we control for age. The lines are essentially parallel.

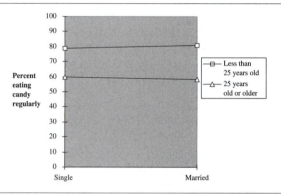

2. *Internal Replication.* This term appears to have been introduced by Hirschi and Selvin (1967). Internal replication occurs when the third variable does not affect the original relationship (see Figures 5.3a, 5.3b, and 5.3c). In this case, we conclude that the third variable is not an important variable in this relationship. Our faith in the original two-variable relationship becomes strengthened because we have ruled out one possible alternative hypothesis.

Figure 5.3a   It appears that heavy TV viewers are more likely to give the TV answer to a survey question than light viewers are. But will this relationship hold up once control variables are introduced?

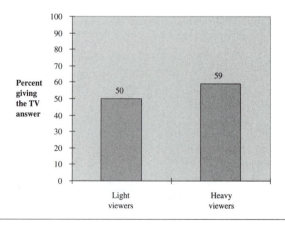

SOURCE: Adapted from G. Gerbner & L. Gross (1976). "Living with television: The violence profile." *Journal of Communication, 26*: 192.

Figure 5.3b   We control for age and find that it has no impact on the original relationship. Heavy TV viewers are more likely to give the TV answer regardless of their age. This is internal replication of the original relationship.

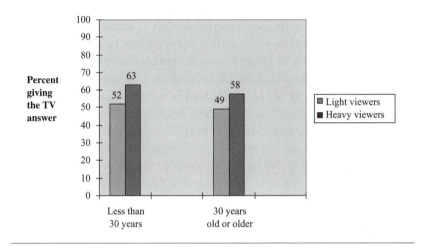

Figure 5.3c   A line graph also shows that the original hypothesis is still supported. The two lines are close together, indicating little or no main effect of age.

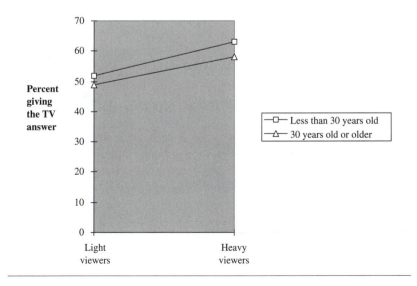

3. *Interpretation.* This is another of the outcomes discussed by Hyman (1955). Interpretation takes place when a third variable occurs in sequence between the independent variable and the dependent variable, and the third variable accounts for the original relationship (see Figures 5.4a, 5.4b, and 5.4c). Interpretation and explanation differ only in the time sequence or causal sequence that is attributed to the variables. If the third or control variable occurs prior to the two original variables, we are in a situation in which explanation might occur. If the third or control variable occurs in a time sequence between the two original variables, we are in a situation in which interpretation might occur. The causal sequence is typically something that the researcher must determine. In many cases, it may be very clear which variable occurs first in a causal sequence, but in other cases it may be a matter of debate. Two factors can be used to help us decide whether one variable is causally prior to another: time order and the fixity or alterability of the variables (Rosenberg, 1968). For example, gender is a fixed or unalterable variable, and it is not likely to have been caused by another variable in a data set, such as voting behavior.

Figure 5.4a   It appears that high-education people are more likely to show high political knowledge than are low-education people (data are hypothetical). But what happens when we introduce control variables?

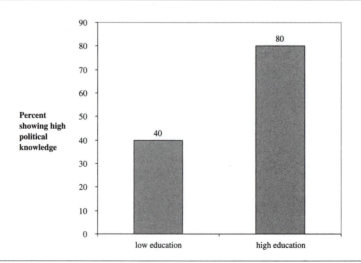

Figure 5.4b   We control for newspaper reading and find that this variable intervenes causally between education and political knowledge, making the original relationship disappear. This is a case of interpretation—introducing the proper control variable helps us interpret the original relationship (data are hypothetical).

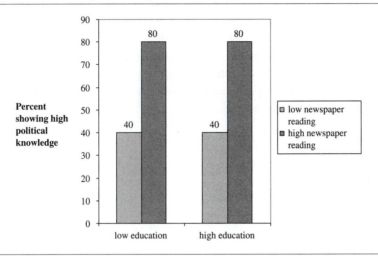

Figure 5.4c   A line graph also shows that newspaper reading is a better predictor of political knowledge than is level of education. There is a main effect of newspaper reading only, and there is no interaction (data are hypothetical).

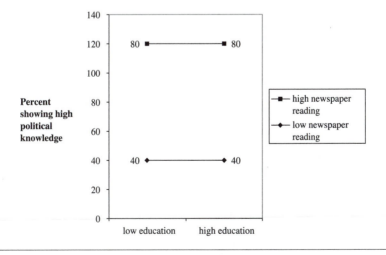

4. *Interaction.* This is a term from analysis of variance meaning that the relationship between one variable and another variable is dependent on the value or level of a third variable (see Figures 5.5a, 5.5b, and 5.5c). This is the frequent situation in social science research that elicits the "it depends" conclusion. This outcome helps the researcher to specify the contingent conditions under which a relationship holds up. Hirschi and Selvin (1967) indicate that this is the most common outcome of introducing a third variable. They point out that Hyman (1955) used the term *specification* for a particularly strong interaction—one in which one partial relationship is stronger than the original relationship, or perhaps opposite in sign.

Figure 5.5a   It appeared in these data from the 1980s that people higher in education were more likely to favor a nuclear freeze than were people lower in education. Is this a genuine relationship, or is it spurious?

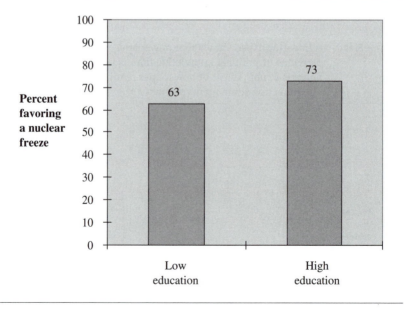

SOURCE: Adapted from J. W. Tankard, Jr. (1983, August). *Knowledge and opinion on the nuclear freeze: A test of three models.* Paper presented to the Communication Theory and Methodology Division, Association for Education in Journalism and Mass Communication, Corvallis, Oregon.

Figure 5.5b   Introducing political orientation as a third variable shows an interaction—the relationship between the original two variables depends on the value of the third variable. For conservatives, the difference in education makes little difference. For liberals, the difference in education makes a substantial difference.

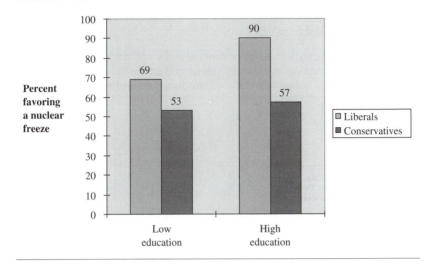

Figure 5.5c   A line graph also illustrates the interaction. Line graphs are very useful for detecting and illustrating interactions. If the two lines are not parallel, this indicates that an interaction is present. If the two lines are parallel, there is no interaction.

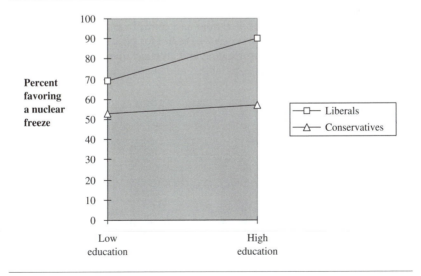

5. *Additivity.* This occurs when both the independent variable and the control variable affect the dependent variable, but the effects are independent and the variables do not interact (see Figures 5.6a, 5.6b, and 5.6c). In the terms of analysis of variance, this is the situation in which you have two main effects but no interaction. This is the outcome that, although quite common, has tended to be overlooked in some discussions of three-variable relationships.

Figure 5.6a   It appears that heavy viewers of TV are more likely to give the TV answer to a survey question than are light viewers. But what happens when we introduce a control variable?

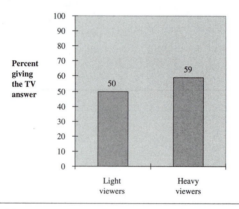

SOURCE: Adapted from G. Gerbner & Larry Gross (1976). Living with television: The violence profile. *Journal of Communication, 26,* 192.

Figure 5.6b   After we introduce gender as a control variable, the results show additivity. When we control for gender, we see an effect due to television viewing and an effect due to gender. The effects of the two variables "add" up.

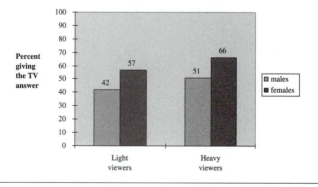

Figure 5.6c   Again, presenting the results in a line graph often makes it easier for us to understand the relationship. We see main effects of gender and TV viewing, but the parallel lines tell us there is no interaction.

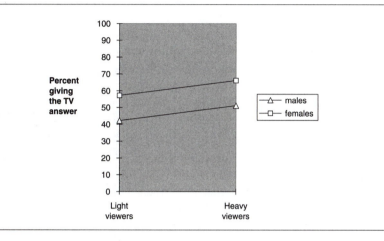

❖ PROPER FORM FOR HYPOTHESES

The recommendation of studying three-variable relationships raises an important question—what is the proper form of hypotheses for three-variable relationships? In Hage's terms, this is the question of the operational linkage.

Three-variable hypotheses frequently express relationships that are so complicated that they are difficult to put into words. In addition, they are often poorly stated. Eveland (1997) noted that key phrases in statements suggesting interactions (and nonlinearity) include *will depend on, will be different for, should increase the effect,* and *will occur only for* (p. 405). But, hypotheses using these phrases may not be clear or specific enough.

The statement by Gerbner, Gross, Morgan, and Signorielli (1980) of their "mainstreaming" hypothesis shows how confusing statements of three-variable relationships can be: "By 'mainstreaming' we mean the sharing of that commonality among heavy viewers in those demographic groups whose light viewers hold divergent views" (p. 15). This is three-variable hypothesis, with the phrase *demographic groups* covering a number of different possible third variables. But it is difficult to draw in advance the bar chart that would illustrate a result that would fit the hypothesis.

A well-known hypothesis that illustrates the complexity of three-variable relationships is the knowledge gap hypothesis. As stated in the original article by Tichenor et al. (1970), this hypothesis takes the following form:

> As the infusion of mass media information into a social system increases, segments of the population with higher socioeconomic status tend to acquire this information at a faster rate than the lower status segments, so that the gap in knowledge between these segments tends to increase rather than decrease. (p. 159)

This statement of the knowledge gap hypothesis is probably about as clear as it can be, but it is noteworthy that it is 49 words long and that a diagram is almost necessary to show just what is meant.

Several forms of hypotheses that we sometimes see presented do not seem to be adequate. For instance, it is not enough to predict that "there will be an interaction." A number of different patterns of interaction are possible, and this kind of statement does not specify which one.

An example given by Hage (1972) also does not seem to suggest a workable general form for a three-variable hypothesis. Hage presented this hypothesis: "The lower the education, when there is little or no income, the lower the power (p. 94)." But this statement leaves out half of the full three-variable table—the half corresponding to the condition of high income.

What seems to be needed in a hypothesis for a three-variable relationship is a very explicit statement of the expected relationship between Variables X and Y for each condition of Variable Z. The hypothesis can almost mirror the form of a table showing a three-variable relationship. For instance, here is an explicit statement of the kind of prediction one might make for a well-known attitude change experiment:

> When audience members are high in education, a two-sided message will lead to more attitude change than a one-sided message, but when audience members are low in education, a two-sided message will lead to less attitude change than a one-sided message.

The above hypothesis is also somewhat long, but such length may be necessary to deal with the complexity of a three-variable relationship.

❖ SOME METHODOLOGICAL CONSIDERATIONS

Three-variable analysis is a strategy that is applicable with many research methods, including particularly surveys and experiments. It may also be suitable in content analysis research if the object of the content analysis is to test hypotheses about causal relationships.

Various techniques of data presentation and analysis can be used to carry out three-variable analyses. This chapter has stressed visual examination of three-variable relationships with column charts and line graphs. Such visual techniques present some obvious advantages in presenting relationships clearly (Tankard, 1994). Gerbner and his associates in their research on television have used column charts for much of their data presentation (Gerbner & Gross, 1976; Gerbner et al., 1980). Three-variable relationships can also be presented in the form of cross-tabulation tables, and this was the technique used predominantly by such pioneers as Lazarsfeld and Hyman.

Other techniques that can be used to examine three-variable relationships include partial correlation, factorial designs using analysis of variance, and looking at correlation coefficients within subgroups. An example of the last technique is O'Keefe's (1985) study of the effectiveness of a mass media crime prevention program. This technique has some of the advantages of partial correlation—there are fewer numbers to look at in a table, and the computer can do a lot of the work for you—and some of the advantages of cross-tabulations—you can see which of the five types of three-variable relationships you have.

If a researcher is going to attempt three-variable analysis, one of the important questions becomes which variables to use as control variables. The primary criterion for selection of control variables should be theoretical relevance (Rosenberg, 1968, p. 38). Is the control variable likely to be implicated in the relationship? In most situations, there will be numerous variables that one could select as a third variable, with several purposes in theory building that could be served by selecting each. So the process of selecting control variables should not be a mindless one, and it requires some knowledge of theory.

Finally, a few methodological warnings seem in order for researchers working on three-variable relationships. As more analysis by subgroups is done, replication probably becomes more important, to show that differences between subgroups aren't due merely to sampling error. Also, there is another danger in looking at differences between subgroups—the danger of post hoc reasoning. One of the problems with post hoc reasoning is that it can mean that nothing is ever falsified. Instead of falsifying a hypothesis, we qualify it. For instance, a researcher might start out with a hypothesis that a certain general effect will occur. In various studies of the hypothesis, however, it might happen that the hypothesis is supported in some studies whereas its logical opposite is supported in other studies. The tendency in these cases seems to be not to conclude that there is evidence contrary to the original hypothesis but to revise it to state that the outcome is dependent on a third variable. Although this procedure is essentially the approach being presented in this chapter, it does raise some questions. Falsification, as used by Popper (1959), and strong inference, as used by Platt (1964), do not seem possible with this approach.

❖ CONCLUSION

The main purpose of this chapter is to extend our thinking in theory building beyond two-variable relationships to three-variable relationships. The chapter points out that introducing third variables into an analysis can serve several important purposes in theory building beyond just checking for a spurious relationship.

Much of social science theory seems to be moving toward a shift from statements of very general relationships between two variables to more qualified statements of when effects are likely to occur. In general, we're moving away from strong effects models of human behavior and toward contingent effects models. The conclusions we are reaching seem to be similar to the conclusion Roger Brown (1958) drew some years ago about the effectiveness of the propaganda devices—that they are "contingently rather than invariably effective" (p. 306).

Three-variable analysis is highly suitable for this kind of theory development. It seems to be the next logical step beyond the two-variable approach.

6

Theoretical Statements Relating Four or More Variables

In this chapter, we cover why the theory builder might want to use more than three variables in a hypothesis and how to construct theoretical statements relating four or more variables. We will learn how to extend the three-variable strategy to these more complex systems, how to express such multivariate relationships in hypothesis form, and how to think about theoretical and operational linkages for the multivariate relationships of complex systems.

In building theory, the importance of well-expressed theoretical statements cannot be overemphasized. If formulated properly, theoretical statements help the theory builder stay focused on the task at hand. An added benefit is that clear theoretical statements help communicate to others what one is attempting to do. As we have seen, even the study of how one concept is related to another concept can be sidetracked by a poorly conceived theoretical statement. As we also have seen, the addition of just one more concept to our theory will significantly increase the complexity of our work, making it all the more important to produce statements that help us to be clear about what we are doing and to communicate that clearly to others.

Theory builders in the social sciences often are placed in the awkward position of knowing that their theorizing may be too simple to reflect reality accurately but also too complicated to allow realistic investigations. Faced with this dilemma—the complexities of human behaviors and the limitations of human minds—the theory builder faces difficult choices. The suggestion is often made that the theory builder start simply and then add complexity as the need warrants. The problem arises when one fails to recognize when things have become too complex. This is precisely the point at which the value of theoretical statements fully manifests.

❖ FORMULATING THEORETICAL STATEMENTS FOR COMPLEX SYSTEMS

Let's suppose that we have established the relationship between two concepts and that we have felt comfortable enough to introduce a third concept to our model of social life. In Chapter 5, we discussed at length the reasons for doing so and the ways to do it. Generally, our goal is to state the expected relationship between an independent variable and a dependent variable for each condition of the third variable and to look for any changes produced. McCombs and Shaw (1972), for example, proposed and began to demonstrate that the *press agenda*—the set of political issues the news media cover most assiduously—affects the *public agenda*—the set of political issues the public considers most important. As the press agenda changes, they said, the public agenda follows. Here we have a theoretical statement causally linking two variables. The hunch here is that the public agenda depends on the press agenda.

Additional studies presented problems, however. Whereas some studies found media agenda-setting effects, others did not. Efforts to reconcile the conflicting findings met with some success when Zucker (1978) suggested that media agenda setting would depend on how much a particular political issue intruded into the public's everyday life. For issues like inflation, he said, the public does not need guidance from the media to know that it is or is not an important concern. Trips to the grocery store and the gas station tell us whether prices are stable or not. Therefore, the media do not affect the public agenda much when it comes to "obtrusive issues." However, for issues with which the public has little direct experience, such as a foreign conflict, the media are likely to have an agenda-setting effect. Zucker's introduction of a critical third variable into the agenda-setting equation—*issue obtrusiveness*—thus helped advance our understanding of agenda-setting processes and effects.

Here, issue obtrusiveness becomes a contingent condition in the agenda-setting process. How might we state the hypothesis that expresses the expected relationships among the three variables? Here is one such theoretical statement:

> Press coverage of obtrusive political issues has no effect on the issues' salience to the public; however, the greater the press coverage of an unobtrusive political issue, the more salient that issue becomes to the public, whereas the lesser the press coverage of an unobtrusive political issue, the less salient that issue becomes to the public.

Notice that this theoretical statement addresses all of the possible conditions of each of the three variables. Again, the general procedure for introducing a third concept into a simpler model of social life is to state the hypothesized relationship between the independent variable (e.g., the *press agenda*) and the dependent variable (the *public agenda*) for each value of the third variable (*issue obtrusiveness*) and then to look for any changes produced.

Compared to some other scientific fields, however, communication research has been rather slow in developing this procedure for building theory. What might be called a paradigm shift occurred in communication research in the last quarter of the 20th century. The word *paradigm* is often used to refer to the general way of doing things at any one time within a scientific discipline. A paradigm shifts when enough scientists working within that discipline recognize that the way they have been doing things is inadequate for dealing with the complexities they want to study, and a new set of norms emerges to displace the old one (Kuhn, 1970). Thus, in the middle of the second half of the 20th century, many communication scholars began to move beyond the study of so-called "main effects" to the study of so-called "conditional effects." Instead of studying merely the effect of an independent variable on a dependent variable, they began to study routinely the effect of third variables on the original main relationship (Roberts & Maccoby, 1985).

However, building theory is not and has never been a matter of simply shoveling more variables into studies. At about the same time that communication research was discovering the need to study conditional variables, the more established discipline of social psychology, which had been fascinated by intervening processes and other conditional effects for years (Chaffee, 1977), was undergoing a paradigm shift of its own. In that older, more developed discipline, scholars were beginning to question seriously the simple linear process model altogether, arguing that both the cognitive system and the social system are inadequately described as a sequential chain of cause and effect. As McGuire (1973) put it,

> Simple *a*-affects-*b* hypotheses fail to catch the complexities of parallel processing, bidirectional causality, and reverberating feedback that characterize both cognitive and social organizations. The simple sequential model had its uses, but these have been largely exploited in past progress, and we must now deal with the complexities of systems in order to continue the progress on a new level. (p. 37)

Suppose we have a theory that relates six concepts. If we consider all the possible bivariate combinations among these six variables, then there are 15 theoretical statements that can be made. If we think time order matters, as we often do, then there are 30. Fortunately, not all of these will be equally probable. As Hage (1972) observed, perhaps "theory begins when we say some combinations do not occur" (p. 56).

With the introduction of each new concept, the theory builder should state the expected relationship between the independent variable and the dependent variable for each condition of the new variable. If our ideas are good, we will be able to articulate a theoretical statement that captures them. If our ideas are faulty, this exercise will expose them. Either way, we will have made progress.

Although a theoretical statement expressing a three-variable hypothesis is considerably longer and more complex than a theoretical statement expressing a two-variable hypothesis, when we move to a four-variable hypothesis the complexity and length become even greater. What might such a theoretical statement look like? Consider Hovland's careful and systematic work on attitude change (Hovland, Janis, & Kelley, 1953; Hovland, Lumsdaine, & Sheffield, 1949). A number of his experiments examined whether a one-sided or a two-sided message would be more effective. A one-sided message includes only favorable arguments, whereas a two-sided message includes the opposition's arguments, which are then refuted. Hovland wondered whether the relative effectiveness of a one- or two-sided message might depend upon two important audience factors—education and initial favorability toward the message. He thought that the more highly educated audience members, as well as those initially opposed to the message, might respond better to a two-sided message because they would be more likely to be aware of and to think about the counterarguments. Here, we have four variables: (a) the nature of the message, in terms of its being either one-sided or two-sided; (b) the amount of attitude change, in terms of movement closer to or away from the targeted message; (c) the audience's education level, whether relatively high or low; and (d) the audience's initial position, whether initially favorable or initially opposed to the target message. How might we state the proposed relationships among these four variables? Here is a theoretical statement that adequately captures this four-variable hypothesis:

When audience members are high in education and initially opposed, a two-sided message will lead to more attitude change than a one-sided message, but when audience members are low in education and initially favorable, a two-sided message will lead to less attitude change than a one-sided message, and when audience members are either high in education and initially favorable or low in education and initially opposed, a two-sided message will lead to about the same attitude change as will a one-sided message.

By producing a comprehensive theoretical statement, one that "covers all the bases," we are indicating that we have a clear understanding of how we think these variables are related. Note, for example, that the theoretical statement implies that the two audience factors of education and initial favorability are independent: that is, that they are not related to each other. Furthermore, it implies that their effects on attitude change are relatively equal and can thus cancel each other out. If we were unable or unwilling to make such assumptions, the theoretical statement would be even more complicated.

❖ VISUALIZING FOUR-VARIABLE RELATIONSHIPS

At this point, the value of graphic presentations of our ideas becomes clear. Such representations can help us understand and communicate more easily the possible outcomes of the observations we would make to test our theoretical statements. We should face it: Four-variable relationships *are* going to be hard to understand, at least at first, until we become thoroughly familiar with them. One way to make them less forbidding is to sketch the possible outcomes graphically. Although bar charts and other graphic representations may be useful, perhaps the easiest illustrative technique to use is the line graph, for it can show us very clearly and simply how three, four, and even more variables are related. Earlier, we showed how the theory builder can effectively use line charts to describe clearly the possible results of theoretical statements relating two and three variables. Now we will see how we can extend that practice to more complicated systems.

Suppose we are interested in exploring the relationship between television viewing and crime fear, as Gerbner and Gross (1976) did in their cultivation theory. We can begin by roughly dividing subjects into two categories, based on the dependent variable. Thus, we can separate those with relatively high crime fears from those with relatively low crime fears. We can do this in a number of ways, but one common approach is to calculate the mean level of crime fear and to put those with higher levels into one group and the rest into the other group. We then can go through the same process for the primary independent variable, *amount of television viewing,* creating two categories of relatively light and heavy viewers. Using the standard format of plotting the dependent variable Y on the *y* axis and the primary independent variable X on the *x* axis, we can see the effect of X on Y clearly.

Suppose that in the group of light TV viewers, 67 percent have a relatively low fear of crime and 33 percent have a high fear of crime and that in the group of relatively heavy TV viewers, 25 percent have a relatively low fear of crime and 75 percent have a relatively high fear of crime. A line chart showing the relationship between these two variables might look something like the one in Figure 6.1.

Because the line from low to high levels of crime fear is not parallel to the *x* axis but slanted, it shows that there is indeed a relationship between these two variables.

Of course, just because we have observed a relationship between two variables does not mean that one necessarily causes the other. For one thing, what we think is the cause may in fact be the effect (i.e., reverse causality). In other words, how can we be sure that TV viewing leads to crime fear rather than the other way around?

Figure 6.1   Bivariate relationship between TV viewing and crime fear

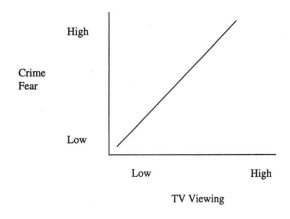

To do that, we should demonstrate that the presumed independent variable (*TV viewing*) precedes the presumed dependent variable (*crime fear*) in time. Furthermore, even after we have established the correct time ordering of the variables, how can we be sure that there is not some other factor that is causing both TV viewing and crime fear? We may never be sure of this, but we can try our best to eliminate all of the possible factors that come to mind. By eliminating these alternative explanations, we strengthen our original argument.

For example, is it not at least feasible that education might drive both TV viewing and crime fear? Perhaps those with high education watch less television and also have less fear of crime. To test this challenge to cultivation theory, Gerbner and Gross examined the effect of this "third variable" of *education* (as well as others, such as *income*) on the original relationship they found between TV viewing and crime fear.

To examine the effect of a third variable, we can subdivide the sample once more into those with relatively low levels of the third variable and those with relatively high levels. Then we examine how these two lines are related, and that tells us how the third variable is related to the original two variables. There are four possibilities.

First, we might find that the two lines closely resemble the one line we saw in the original two-variable case: That is, the two lines, one representing high levels of the third variable and the other

Figure 6.2   Three-variable relationship between TV viewing, education, and crime fear

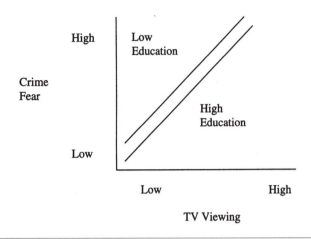

representing low levels, incline in the same direction and at roughly the same angle, running basically parallel to each other. Furthermore, let's say the two lines are relatively close together. The line chart showing this relationship among these three variables might look like the one in Figure 6.2.

Because the two lines maintain roughly the same angle as the first, because they are parallel to each other and because they are close to each other, we can see that the original relationship between viewing and fear holds and that education does not play a major role. This is *internal replication*.

A second possibility is that the two lines still form an incline and are still roughly parallel to each other but that there is a relatively large gap between the two lines. In other words, this line chart looks very much like the previous one except that in the earlier case the two lines were close to each other and in this case they are not. Let's assume the third variable is *gender*. The line chart showing the relationship among these three variables might look something like the one in Figure 6.3.

As in the first case, the two lines maintain roughly the same angle as the line in the original two-variable chart, and they also are parallel to each other, but there is one important difference. Here,

Figure 6.3   Three-variable relationship between TV viewing, gender, and crime fear

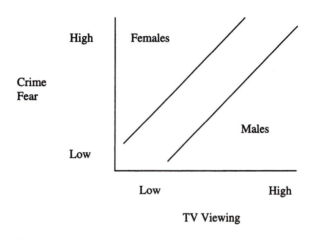

there is a considerable gap between the two lines. This tells us that the original relationship continues to hold—that is, viewing and fear are related—but that gender has an effect, as well. This is what we referred to in Chapter 5 as *additivity*. Each independent variable adds to the effect on the dependent variable.

Third, we could find that the two lines are no longer roughly parallel to each other: That is, that they are closer together at one end and further apart at the other end. Let's assume we control for political ideology. The line chart showing this relationship among these three variables might look something like the one in Figure 6.4.

The lack of parallelism between the two lines tells us that there is an interaction between the third variable and the other two variables. In the example, the original relationship between viewing and fear holds for liberals, but it disappears for conservatives. This is what we referred to in Chapter 5 as an *interaction*.

A fourth possibility is that after we control for a third variable, the two lines representing the relationships among the three variables are now roughly parallel to each other and also roughly parallel to the *x* axis. A pattern like this has two possible meanings, depending upon how the theory builder imagines the three variables to be arranged in order of time, or causally. Let's assume the third variable we are controlling for is

Figure 6.4   Three-variable relationship between TV viewing, political ideology, and crime fear

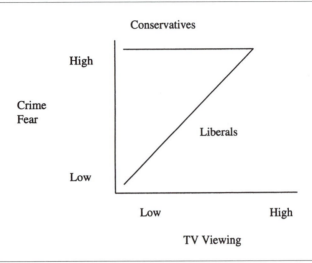

neighborhood crime. The line chart showing this relationship among these three variables might look something like the one in Figure 6.5.

Because both lines are parallel to the *x* axis, we can see that the original relationship has disappeared and that the relationship between viewing and fear can be explained away by considering neighborhood crime. This is what we referred to in Chapter 5 as either *explanation* or *interpretation.* Which of the two it is depends on how we think the three variables are time-ordered or causally related. If we think the third variable occurs first in time, before the independent variable, then it is a case of explanation. Because it is more likely that neighborhood crime leads to TV viewing than vice versa, this is an example of explanation.

Suppose, on the other hand, that we get exactly the same pattern in our line chart but that the control variable is lethargy. If we believe that television viewing leads to lethargy, rather than the other way around, this would be an example of what we referred to in Chapter 5 as interpretation. (We will elaborate further on this question of explanation versus interpretation shortly.)

Thus, we can look at a line chart showing the relationships among three variables and quickly tell what's going on. Two parallel lines mean there is no interaction taking place, whereas two nonparallel lines

Figure 6.5   Three-variable relationship between TV viewing, neighborhood crime, and crime fear

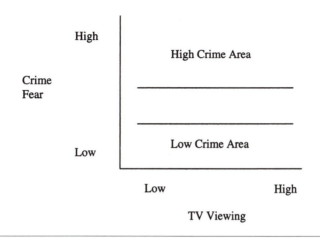

mean there is an interaction. Two close-together parallel lines mean the third variable has no effect on the original relationship, whereas two parallel lines not close together mean that the third variable adds to the explanation or prediction. Finally, two parallel lines that are parallel also to the x axis mean that the original relationship is explained away by the control variable, in a case of either explanation or interpretation, depending on the presumed or known causal ordering or time ordering of the variables. (The case of two close-together parallel lines that are parallel to the x axis will not occur because this presumes a case where the original variables were not found to be related in the first place.)

❖   EXTENDING THE THREE-VARIABLE
     STRATEGY TO COMPLEX SYSTEMS

Now we are ready to extend our analysis to the addition of a fourth variable. Let's assume that we have controlled for every conceivable third variable that we can think of and for which we have measures, and we have found that the relationship between viewing and crime fear holds except that (a) the relationship between viewing and crime fear appears to depend on gender (thus, a case of interaction) and (b) neighborhood crime appears to contribute to crime fear,

Figure 6.6   Three-variable relationship between TV viewing, gender, and crime fear

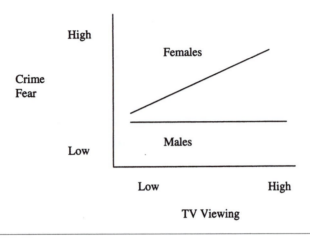

Figure 6.7   Three-variable relationship between TV viewing, neighborhood crime, and crime fear

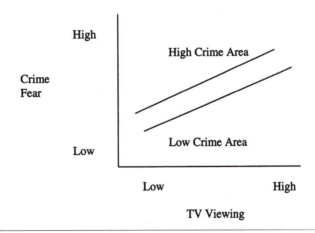

independently of TV viewing (thus, a case of additivity). Line charts graphically illustrating each of these relationships might look something like those shown in Figures 6.6 and 6.7.

Suppose further that we do not have any good reason to expect that level of neighborhood crime is related to gender. In other words,

Figure 6.8   Four-variable relationship between TV viewing, gender, neighborhood crime, and crime fear

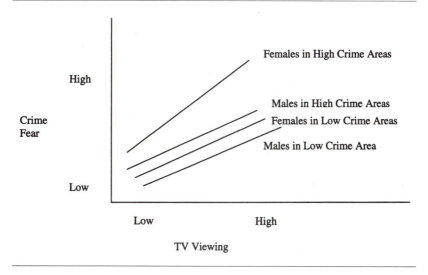

we expect there to be roughly as many women living in high-crime neighborhoods as there are women in low-crime neighborhoods. We could examine U.S. Census Bureau, Justice Department, or other relevant data to confirm or deny this expectation. If we are correct in our assumption, our line chart might look something like the one in Figure 6.8.

Notice that instead of two lines to compare, as in the case of the three-variable relationships, we now have four lines. Notice also, however, that the simplicity of meaning attached to the three-variable charts is lost when we add just one new variable. Even in this simplest of cases, where we are not suggesting any relationship between the two control variables, the patterns we encountered earlier and their simple interpretations break down. The interaction contributed by age interferes with the additivity contributed by neighborhood crime so that the additivity becomes obscured by the interaction. In one sense, the interaction "overrides" the additivity so that what is in reality a case of additivity becomes confounded by the interaction created by gender, even though gender and neighborhood crime are not related to each other.

This example points out how important it is to look at bivariate relationships *separately* before examining trivariate relationships and to examine trivariate relationships *separately* before moving on to even more complicated multivariate relationships. It is crucial that we understand these simpler relationships *before* we attempt to add new variables to the equation.

This example also leads to a second important point. Notice that if we were to attempt to add a fifth variable to the equation, the number of lines necessary to represent such a model would be twice the number in the previous case. Let's assume, for example, that we had reason to believe that political ideology contributed to our explanation or prediction. Besides males in low-crime areas, females in low-crime areas, males in high-crime areas and females in high-crime areas, we would have four additional lines representing each of these for both liberals and conservatives. Furthermore, were we to attempt to add a third value to that new variable (political moderates), the result would be four more lines. Clearly, the line chart would quickly become too complicated to serve its purpose. If we keep the above caveats in mind, we can use line charts to help us keep track of what we are doing and to imagine what the results of empirical tests of our hypotheses might look like.

The approach we have taken here closely corresponds to logical extensions of the basic cross-tabulation of two, three, and four variables. Indeed, it is possible to add additional control variables, as well as additional categories within the variables, to produce contingency tables of even larger sizes. Computer packages make such efforts easy—but only if we understand first what we are doing. Our point, however, is that understanding what we are doing and the techniques described here can help us in that endeavor. Once we have mastered these techniques, we can begin to consider carefully other important issues, such as how strongly any two of the variables are related to each other (measures of association) and the probability that the observed relationship could have happened by chance (tests of statistical significance). Statistics texts treat such issues at length and offer guidance on which particular measures and tests are appropriate for different levels of measurement of the variables studied (see also Appendix B).

❖ ORDERING THE VARIABLES IN TIME

Let us return for a moment to the question of explanation versus interpretation. Again, the line charts cannot tell us which is which. This is because the only difference between explanation and interpretation is our presumption of which variables are causes and which are effects. The line chart can tell us whether a relationship exists (correlation), but it cannot tell us which variables are causes and which are effects. Therefore, the same line chart could show either explanation or interpretation, depending on how we think the variables occur in time. Even when we are dealing with just two variables, the questions of time ordering can be important. Once McCombs and Shaw (1972) showed that the press agenda and the public agenda covaried, their next step was to show that the press agenda leads to the public agenda and not the other way around (Shaw & McCombs, 1977). As we add more variables to our study, the time-ordering question becomes more important.

This brings us to our next important step in theory building with complex systems. Do we understand the approximate time ordering of the variables? We may not be able to achieve a completely unidirectional flow of causality, but for every case in which we establish (or are willing to assume) that Variable X is the cause of Variable Y, and not vice versa, we have greatly simplified our task. If we are able to view the relationships among the set of variables as involving only one-way causation, then we are able to build a model consisting of what is called a recursive system of equations. This can significantly simplify the task of studying four or more variables simultaneously.

Another useful technique that can take us one step further in our attempt to simplify our work is the *block recursive model*, a technique based on the notion that causes and effects in social life can be conceived of as being bundled together (Blalock, 1969). Thus, a "cause" of something may consist of a subset of variables, as may an "effect," and one can then link chains of causes and effects, each of which forms a bivariate block.

Suppose, for example, that one is interested in how news media content happens, and one suspects that among the causes are competition from rival media, community standards, and other variables that are *outside* the production system per se, as well as causes located *inside* the production system, such as staff training and organizational routines. Shoemaker and Reese (1996) proposed a comprehensive hierarchy of such causes of news content, grouping together those that pertain to the individual person, the organization, the nation-state, and so forth. Hage (1972) suggested that variables can often be generally classed in terms of those that are (a) outside the system, (b) resources or inputs of the system, (c) structures of the system, (d) integration processes of the system, (e) performances of the system, and (f) outputs of the system. Groupings of variables such as these will almost always suggest a time ordering. Later, if the need arises, one can begin to consider feedback issues or other complications, but only after one has a firm grasp of the unidirectional model.

This technique may seem onerous and perhaps even needlessly burdensome, but given the difficulty of establishing and understanding how more than two variables might be related, it can prove to be a valuable tool for theory construction.

❖ ANALYZING PATHS AMONG MULTIPLE VARIABLES

A technique known as *path analysis* has become an important tool that enables researchers to explore questions of causation from correlational data. Introduced by Wright (1921) and popularized in the social sciences by Blalock (1964) and Duncan (1966), path analysis has become widely used as a method for inferring time-order relationships from nonexperimental data, such as synchronous (single-wave) surveys. As a result of the development of path analysis and other correlational methods such as cross-lagged correlation, the old argument that one cannot say anything about causation from correlational data is no longer quite true. Path analysis is now routinely employed as a way to test hypotheses dealing with more than two variables over a sequence of time. However, it can also be a valuable tool for theory construction.

Path analysis is based on the general assumption that two events that hypothetically occur in time close to each other will be more strongly related than two events separated by greater time, intervening events, or both. We start with a causal theory that involves more than two variables occurring at more than one time. For example, suppose we think that Variables W, X, and Y cause Variable Z. There are a number of ways in which the three independent variables might relate to Z and to each other. Suppose we think that Variables W, X, and Y are interrelated such that W affects X and Y directly, X does not affect W directly, Y does not affect either W or X directly, and all three directly affect Z. Thus, we might think that political tolerance (Z) is caused by education (W), income (X), and media use (Y). Furthermore, we might think that education affects income and media use directly;

Figure 6.9   Path diagram of education, income, media use, and political
tolerance

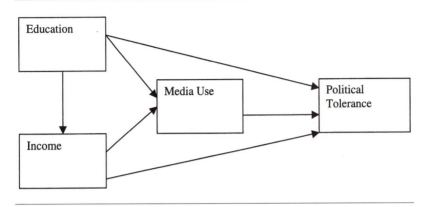

that income does not affect education directly; that media use does not
affect either education or income directly; and that education, income,
and media use all affect political tolerance directly. The path diagram
describing these relationships might look like the one shown in
Figure 6.9.

Such a path model should have a rationale for the linking of each
pair of variables: that is, an explanation in words of why it is believed
that one variable influences the others. Note that this causal theory is
specified first and then path analysis is used to determine if the presumed ordering of these variables is structurally sound. The strength
of the direct and indirect influences that each variable has on the other
variables that follow it is then estimated using multiple regression. In
other words, multiple regression is used here as a descriptive tool. It is
used to describe the structure connecting independent and dependent
variables and to evaluate the logical consequences of a structural
model that has been proposed from some causal theory. It is the theory
that specifies how the variables are ordered. Each arrow in the diagram
represents a presumed causal linkage or path of causal inference
between each pair of variables. The strength of each separate path is
then estimated through the use of multiple regression. The estimation
will actually involve several regression equations, depending upon the
number of variables, and variables that are independent in one equation may be dependent variables in another. For example, here *income*
is a dependent variable for the education-income relationship, *media*

use is a dependent variable for the education-income-media use relationship, and, finally, *political tolerance* is a dependent variable for the entire structure.

A strength of this approach to theory building is that it forces us to think about how the variables in the system are connected. Which variables have a causal influence on which other variables, and which way does the causal influence flow? In drawing a picture of a path model, one is required to think about such questions.

It should be noted, however, that because path analysis uses multiple regression to describe the structure among the variables, all of the assumptions of multiple regression still apply, such as the assumptions that the variables are linearly related and that their effects are additive. It is here that the would-be theory builder may get into some trouble because the variables may not be linearly related and the effects may not be additive. As Hage (1972) put it, "The difficulty with machine solutions, especially current regression techniques, is that we are likely to remain at the level of adding variables together instead of specifying nonlinear relationships such as curvilinear or power forms" (p. 88).

Before we assume that the bivariate relationship between Variables X and Y is linear and that the combined effects of the independent variables are additive, it is therefore a good idea to consider how else the variables might be connected. Because nearly all humans efficiently communicate with words, it makes good sense to discuss verbally how we think the variables are connected or at least how they could be connected. Once we have expressed a clear theoretical statement, one that specifies how we think the variables are connected, the next step is to articulate why we think they might be connected in these ways. Why do we think that Variable X causes Variables Y and Z, and why do we think that Variable Y causes Variable Z? Why do we think these variables are linked? If one reviews the social science literature carefully, one will be surprised to see how often studies fail to express clearly why the author thinks each variable being studied is related to the other relevant variables. If we are building theory, we need to identify the variables we think are connected, define them, and show why we think they are connected. Literature reviews also reveal that studies often express how the author thinks each variable is related to the other relevant variables but not why they are related in these ways. In such cases, the author is providing operational linkages but not theoretical ones. We need both.

❖ SPECIFYING NONLINEAR
RELATIONSHIPS AND NONADDITIVE EFFECTS

If we are proposing a theory that includes four concepts, we need to define each of these four concepts (i.e., give conceptual definitions), express relationships between and among these concepts (i.e., provide a theoretical statement), describe how we think the four concepts are related (i.e., provide operational linkages), and describe why we think they are related (i.e., provide theoretical linkages). Starting with a basic bivariate relationship, we work our way up step by step to the complete four-variable system. For example, if we think television viewing affects crime fear, we need to define television watching and crime fear and to state explicitly a theoretical statement, such as "As the amount of television watching increases, the amount of crime fear increases." We then need to articulate how we think television watching affects crime fear (operational linkages), and why (theoretical linkages). Why do we think television viewing affects crime fear? Suppose we think that television's constant underlying message is that certain groups (e.g., women, minorities, the young, the old, the poor) tend to be victims in a violent, crime-ridden world. We think that television generally makes viewers more fearful of crime than they otherwise would be. We also think that those in particular social groups that are often depicted as victims of violence and crime are going to be especially affected: That is, they will become particularly fearful. These and other ideas underlie Gerbner's theory of cultivation (Gerbner & Gross, 1976).

By articulating not just that television viewing is related to crime fear but how we think television viewing is related to crime fear, we begin to recognize that some of these relationships might not be simply linear and that the effects of some of these variables may not be simply additive. For example, it makes sense to wonder how we think the level of crime fear would be affected by heavy television viewing by a poor minority woman, compared to a rich minority woman. Do we think heavy viewing by segments of society that are constantly depicted on television as victims is exponentially affected if they are in two of the designated groups? What if they are in three of the groups? How do we think rich white men living in low-crime areas are affected? Does heavy television viewing *decrease* their crime fears? Why or why not?

As we saw in earlier chapters, two other common ways variables are connected are curvilinear and power forms. If we think the young and the old are disproportionately depicted as victims on television and that consequently young and old viewers are particularly affected by television viewing, then we are maintaining that the relationship between age and crime fear is curvilinear. In other words, as age increases, crime fear at first increases, then decreases, and finally increases again. Likewise, if we think that crime fear generally increases with increases in television viewing but that for certain groups depicted as victims the effect is especially strong, then we might consider the effect to be exponential for members of these groups. This would be a power function. Thus, before making the assumption that the relationship between variables is linear, the theory builder should take the extra step of considering whether one of these other forms is more plausible. Good theoretical linkages will go a long way toward resolving such a question.

We should also not ignore the possibility that the form of the relationship that best matches our theoretical statement is a combination of more than one of the basic forms. For example, we might add two or more curve functions together to produce a wave that represents cycles of economic growth, or we could combine a curvilinear and a power function that shows cycles that are also geometrical. Another common occurrence is having one variable affect another only after a certain threshold is reached, at which point a plateau is reached, and the impact of X on Y only occurs again when a subsequent threshold is reached. For example, suppose we think that education has an effect on social networking but that the relationship is a not simple linear one, such that a unit increase in education leads to a unit increase in networking. Education might be measured in terms of years of schooling, but we might think that the change from Year 8 to Year 9 or the change from Year 12 to Year 13 produces significantly more change than the change from Year 3 to Year 4 or from Year 13 to Year 14. In other words, we might think that the change from primary school to high school and the change from high school to college may produce more change in networking than the change from the third grade to the fourth or from being a college sophomore to being a college junior. We are describing what is known as a step function, which is a basic linear relationship with the addition of incremental limits at certain key points. This variation on the basic linear form is probably more common than many other possible forms of relationships, but unless the theory builder considers it as a possibility it will tend to be ignored.

❖ CAVEATS AND CONCLUSIONS

Generally, we always should look for the most parsimonious ways to describe how we think our concepts are connected, but we should not ignore the possibility that the relationship is not a simple one. Armed with a good theoretical statement and good theoretical linkages, we can make the task of producing good operational linkages much less daunting.

Furthermore, we are addressing here the use of path analysis in theory building and not theory testing. A disadvantage of path models is that they can lead people to think that causal relationships have been demonstrated when in fact they have only been assumed. Unless a path model is tested with data from a panel study or some other source of information with more than one time point, it is not capable of detecting causal direction. Using path analysis to build theory is a form of what is known as the "hypothetico-deductive method." McGuire (1973) described this as a

> creative procedure . . . where one puts together a number of commonsensical principles and derives from their conjunction some interesting predictions, as in the Hull and Hovland *mathematico-deductive* theory of rote learning, or the work by Simon and his colleagues on logical reasoning. (p. 41)

Computers make it feasible to conduct ambitious simulations that make path analysis a theory-building procedure that is both practical and judicious in a wide variety of contexts. However, this use of path analysis contrasts sharply with a theory-free inductive search for the single "best fit" model. Computers also make it feasible to run a large series of tests for many possible models linking a large set of variables. However, such an endeavor is not scientifically sound. A path analysis, like experimentation, should begin with a set of integrated theoretical propositions about the relationships among some variables. These propositions may then be tested as a set with empirical data. That a particular path model fits well with the data does not preclude the possibility that other theoretical models linking the same variables also accord well with empirical findings. The same, however, is true of an experiment. That an experiment's results support a theory does not preclude the possibility that another theory accounts even better for the findings. This better theory, however, will not be found lurking in data. It must be formulated. In the same way, a good path analysis will not magically emerge from data. It, too, must be formulated.

This chapter has attempted to provide the theory builder with sound procedures for advancing theory. Though they may at first appear daunting, they can, with a bit of patience and practice, free the theory builder to develop more sophisticated, imaginative, and important ideas that more closely resemble the complex social world in which we live. Hage (1972), one of the pioneers in the promotion of these ideas to whom we are greatly in debt for much of what we know about theory building in the social sciences, called the suggestions he made for advancing theory "guidelines for our thought processes" (p. 109). Armed with these guidelines, the theory builder can go a long way toward making the social world easier to understand and therefore more pleasant to inhabit.

7

Theoretical Models

A theoretical model is a tool that can promote theory construction. In this chapter, we discuss what a model is and how it can be used to improve theory, including how to represent theories in model form and how to derive theoretical statements from models. Along the way, we look at different types of models, how to evaluate models, and future directions in model building, all in an effort to show how models can be a major implement in the theory builder's toolkit. We will use a variety of models of the communication process to help illustrate our points, which apply equally well to model building throughout the social sciences.

❖ WHAT A MODEL IS

Referring to the use of the word *model* in the social science literature, Kaplan (1964b) noted "the confusing and often confused usage of the term" (p. 267). Sometimes the term is used to refer to a strictly "physical model," such as a wind tunnel. Sometimes it is used to refer to "any theory . . . presented with some degree of mathematical exactness and logical rigor" (p. 267). In such a case, the terms *model* and *theory* are being used simply as synonyms for each other. Sometimes the word is used to represent "a model *of* a theory which presents the latter purely as a structure of uninterpreted symbols," what Kaplan called a "formal model" (p. 267). Perhaps the most famous formal model of all time is the exquisitely simple yet profoundly revealing $E = MC^2$, representing the equivalence of energy and matter that underlies Einstein's theory of relativity. Sometimes the term is used for "presenting a conceptual analogue to some subject-matter," what Kaplan called a "semantical model" (p. 267). This is perhaps the most common usage of the term in the social sciences.

Neuliep (1996) suggested that we distinguish between "scale models" and "conceptual models" (p. 30). A scale model replicates an object from which it differs only in size. A conceptual model involves a change in medium and often is quite abstract as it attempts to represent physical, psychological, and logical processes. Neuliep noted that "because communication is a psychological process, communication models are conceptual models" (p. 30).

There are two useful modifications we might make to Neuliep's definitions. First, let's make a distinction, not between scale models and conceptual models, but between physical models and conceptual models. Most of us were made familiar with physical models in our childhood, when we played with miniature airplanes and miniature kitchen ovens. A scale model is a type of physical model that differs from that which it models only in size. Though many physical models do differ in size from that which they model, they also differ in other ways. For example, a model of a ship may be smaller than that which it models, but it also may lack working sails, engines, rudders, or other essential parts of a full-scale ship. It is a physical model but not a scale model.

Second, though most communication models are conceptual rather than physical in nature, some communication models *are* physical. For example, an enlarged model of the human mouth and throat might be used to demonstrate principles of speech. Likewise, a miniature model of a classroom might be used to demonstrate how seating arrangements affect communication patterns. If this model differs from an actual classroom only in size, it is a scale model as well as a physical one.

Therefore, we may have a communication model that is strictly a physical model, and if it differs from that which it models only in size, then it also is a scale model. Most social science models, however, are not physical but conceptual. In fact, most definitions of the term *model* found in the social science literature indicate their conceptual nature:

Deutsch (1952): A model is "a structure of symbols and operating rules which is supposed to match a set of relevant points in an existing structure or process" (p. 357).

Bill and Hardgrave (1973): "A model is a theoretical and simplified representation of the real world. It is an isomorphic construction of reality or anticipated reality" (p. 28).

McQuail and Windahl (1993): "For our purpose, we consider a model as a consciously simplified description in graphic form of a piece of reality. A model seeks to show the main elements of any structure or process and the relationships between these elements" (p. 2).

Wallace (1994): "Modeling is the process of developing and providing an abstraction of reality, i.e., a model" (p. 1).

Baran and Davis (1995): "Any representation of a system, whether in words or diagrams, is a *model*" (p. 251).

Neuliep (1996): "A model is a graphic representation of an object or process" (p. 29).

Though at first glance there might appear to be significant differences across these six definitions, they are due mainly to the decision to limit the term for some reason. For example, Neuliep (1996) and McQuail and Windahl (1993) imposed the restriction that the model be in graphic form, whereas Baran and Davis (1995) chose to emphasize that a model can be verbal, as well. Lasswell (1948) presented what many communication students regard as one of the earliest and most influential communication models, writing that "a convenient way to describe an act of communication is to answer the following questions:

Who

Says What

In Which Channel

To Whom

With What Effect?" (p. 117).

Baran and Davis (1995) considered this a "model" of the communication process (p. 253), whereas McQuail and Windahl (1993) considered it a "formula" that could be "transformed" into a model by drawing boxes around "Who," and "Says What," and so forth, labeling each box as "Communicator," "Message," and so forth, and then drawing arrows from one box to the next (p. 13; see Figure 7.1).

However, far more impressive than the differences among these definitions are their similarities. There is general agreement that a model applies to an object or a process. That which is modeled also is sometimes referred to as a system or structure. For example, we could have models of two different classroom structures, one suitable for a small graduate seminar and another for a large undergraduate lecture course. We also could have models of the communication processes that predominate in each of these different structures or systems. Thus, feedback might be a more prominent feature of a model of a small seminar course than of a large lecture course.

There also is general agreement that a model is a simplified representation (abstractions being by definition simplifications). Although only Bill and Hardgrave's (1973) definition explicitly refers to the representation as being isomorphic, meaning there is a one-to-one correspondence between what is being modeled and the model itself, that is implied in most of the other definitions as well. Thus, an isomorphic map of a college campus, showing its buildings, walkways, roads, parking areas, and other elements, is a model that could be followed to get easily from one place to another.

We might say that a model simply represents a portion of reality, either an object or a process, in such a way as to highlight what are considered to be key elements or parts of the object or process and the connections among them. A model is not a mirror image of reality but merely makes salient certain aspects of reality. A model helps us focus on some parts and connections among those parts while ignoring other parts and connections. It is this simplifying and focusing that makes models particularly valuable as theory-building tools.

Models Versus Theories

As noted earlier, the terms *model* and *theory* are sometimes used as if they were interchangeable. For example, in discussing how theories in the social sciences tend to cover only limited contexts rather than broad, sweeping portions of reality (more characteristic of theories in the natural sciences), Hanneman (1988) states,

Figure 7.1   Lasswell's model of communication

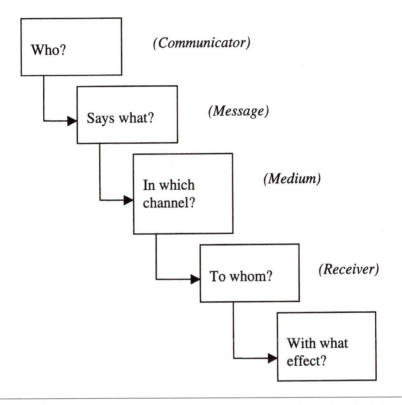

SOURCE: Adapted from Lasswell, 1948, p. 117. Drawn by the authors of this book.

Most social scientists' models deal with particular phenomena, or narrow classes of phenomena. That is, they are theories of the "middle range." Fewer of our models are useful to understanding the similarities and differences across wide ranges of patterns of social behavior. (p. 16)

Here, Hanneman was using *model* and *theory* synonymously, something not all that uncommon in the literature.

Noting that *model* is sometimes used as a synonym for *theory,* Kaplan (1964b) rightly asked, "If 'model' is coextensive with 'theory,' why not just say 'theory'?" (p. 264). The answer is that although they are sometimes confused, there is a good reason to keep the two terms conceptually distinct. A *theory* is a set of systematically related generalizations suggesting new observations for empirical testing. As such, the purpose of a theory is to explain or predict. A *model* does not explain or predict anything. We might say that the purpose of a model is to describe and imagine.

Though a model is not a theory, a model can be used to represent a theory. As Neuliep (1996) noted, "Theorists use models because they can describe and simulate physical, logical, or conceptual processes that may not otherwise be observable or presentable" (p. 30). He gave the example of theories of listening. Because listening is a psychological phenomenon impossible to touch, a model can provide a valuable method of indirect observation. Neuliep stated that models enable theorists to illustrate, delineate, and depict the structural features (i.e., what the object or process looks like—its form) and functional features (i.e., what the object or process actually does—its purpose) of their theories in varying degrees of abstractness and detail. Some models may be very detailed and literal and others rather general and abstract. No matter how detailed or literal a model is, however, it is nothing more than a description of an object or process. If we want to understand how the object or process works, we need something more—a theory.

Even though a model cannot explain or predict, it can help us advance theory. According to Bill and Hardgrave (1973),

> A model, by itself, is not an explanatory device, but it does play an important and directly suggestive role in the formulation of theory. By its very nature it suggests relationships. . . . The jump from a model to a theory is often made so quickly that the model is in fact believed to be a theory. A model is disguised as a theory more often than any other concept. (p. 28)

Actually, a model does more than merely suggest relationships; it *implies* relationships. By making relationships explicit, a model can serve as a useful springboard for theoretical developments. As Deutsch (1952) noted, a model implies judgment of relevance, and that, in turn, implies a theory about the thing modeled. In building a model, a model builder chooses certain elements to include while ignoring others and makes certain connections among elements while ignoring others. These judgments are rarely made in a theoretical vacuum. Often, in fact, theories and models exist in a sort of symbiotic relationship, with theories nourishing models, which may then cultivate theories.

Theories can speak to models, and models can speak to theories. If the dialogue gets frenetic enough, it is sometimes difficult to keep track of the different parties. To put it another way, theories and models can make beautiful music together, and when they dance it is hard to tell which is leading and which is following. If distracted by their skillful teamwork, most people don't really care. As Severin and Tankard (1997) commented, a model "is often confused with theory because the relationship between a model and a theory is so close" (p. 45).

In discussing how theories and models differ, Harvey and Reed (1996) stated:

> Models, as opposed to theories, are well-formed metaphors and analogies. They do not claim to express the truth of the world, but merely to provide heuristic insights. While theories claim to actually explain reality, models are only partial, fictitious constructions. They seek a language of "as if," not "what is." But if models can make few explanatory claims, they are rich in the conceptual materials upon which they can draw and are freer to organize those materials in a manifold of different directions. (p. 309)

Noting that theories are constricted by "a formal operationalist logic or the presuppositions of a well-articulated paradigm," Harvey and Reed pointed out that models are unconstrained by such fetters: "Modeling freely participates in acts of imagination to produce a wide range of alternative insights to old problems" (p. 309). Compared to theories, which tend to be formidable and sometimes even forbidding, models can be more casual than formal and can entice us to toy with them.

Despite their potential playfulness, however, models are serious business. Models help build theory, but they do so mainly by maiming and murdering. Kaplan (1964b) noted that theories and hypotheses often are ill-defined, vague, and uncertain, "at home only in the twilight regions of the mind, where they are safe from sudden exposure" (p. 268). Models, on the other hand, are "conscious, explicit and definite; there is nothing ghostly in their appearance or manner; they look healthy even up to the very moment of their death" (pp. 268-269). In this regard, the model saves us from a certain self-deception: "Forced into the open, our ideas may flutter helplessly; but at least we can see what bloodless creatures they are. As inquiry proceeds, theories must be brought out into the open sooner or later; the model simply makes it sooner" (p. 269).

❖ USES OF MODELS

In discussing what models are and how they differ from theories, we have already touched upon some of the important uses of a model. Deutsch (1952) neatly organized the uses of a model into four different but related functions.

First, a model can help us organize data. It can show similarities and connections among its parts not previously recognized. Because a model is intended to show the major elements of a structure or process and the relationships among them, it can keep us focused on the issues at hand and, at the same time, relate the particulars of our work to that of others working in the same areas but with different models. For example, Lasswell (1948) used his model of an act of communication mentioned earlier to organize the "scientific study of the process of communication" (p. 117). Thus, he stated, the "Who" referred to "control analysis," the "Says What" referred to "content analysis," the "In Which Channel" referred to "media analysis," the "To Whom" referred to "audience analysis," and the "With What Effect" referred to "effect analysis" (p. 117). Lasswell's model of communication thereby served the useful purpose of organizing the study of communication.

Second, a model can help us make predictions. By suggesting relationships we may not have thought about before, a model can lead us to testable hunches. As McQuail and Windahl (1993) noted, a model can "be a basis for assigning probabilities to various alternative outcomes, and hence for formulating hypotheses" (p. 2). They offered a "transmission model of news learning" based on a model of the psychological effects of television viewing on individuals that was originally proposed by Comstock, Chaffee, Katzman, McCombs, and Roberts (1978) (Figure 7.2). This news learning model evoked a number of useful predictions, such as "The probability of a particular item being 'processed' by a receiver as potential information depends on two main factors: its being affectively arousing and attention-gaining; its being selected as relevant or interesting" (McQuail & Windahl, 1993, pp. 86-87). According to this model, much news will be received ("actual exposure"), but it will be "scanned without registering any cognitive or emotional effect" (p. 87). Say McQuail and Windahl, "Audience reach or attention may be recorded, without any process of interpretation taking place. Items which are not processed cannot be comprehended or have learning effects" (p. 87). Just looking at a model and thinking about its parts and connections can generate good hypotheses.

Figure 7.2   McQuail and Windahl's (1993, p. 87) model of news learning, derived from Comstock, Chaffee, Katzman, McCombs, and Roberts's (1978, p. 400) model of the psychological effects of television, and redrawn by the authors of this book.

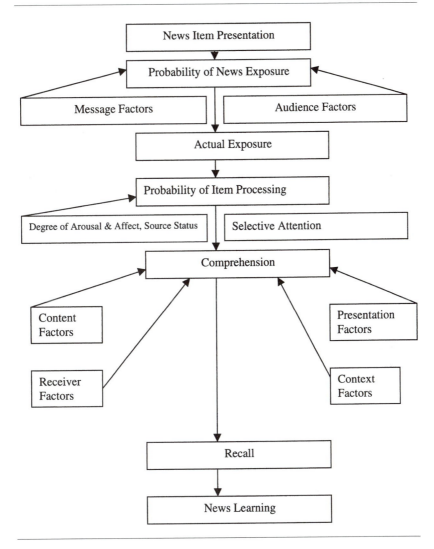

Third, a model can be a helpful heuristic tool, a pedagogical device that encourages students to find out things for themselves. It can be an effective communication device between teacher and student, making complicated and ambiguous information simpler and clearer. Like a good blackboard outline of a class lecture, a model can help students follow material more easily. Noting how science is both a cooperative and a cumulative enterprise, Kaplan (1964b) stated, "The model allows the scientist to make clear to others just what he has in mind" (p. 269). As Holmes and Hundley (1997) noted, "Basic course textbooks usually include communication model illustrations to clarify and reinforce the verbal descriptions" (p. 2).

A course on mass communication theory could be organized in a number of ways. For example, it might be organized along the lines of Lasswell's (1948) model of communication, dealing with the five types of analysis he identified. It also could be organized from the perspective of the mass communicator and could focus on the obstacles he or she faces in trying to reach an audience with a message. These obstacles include properties of the mass communicator, such as lack of journalistic experience, poor language skills, and lack of transmission power, as well as properties of the audience, such as lack of access to the message, selective attention, and selective retention (McCombs & Becker, 1979). A "barriers model of communication" can focus the attention of journalism students on the challenges a journalist faces in trying to reach an audience with an intended message and what the journalist can do to overcome these limitations (Figure 7.3).

Fourth, a model can help us make measurements. As Severin and Tankard (1997) put it, "If the processes that link the model to the thing modeled are clearly understood, the data obtained with the help of a model constitute a measure, whether it be a simple ranking or a full ratio scale" (p. 46). McCombs and Shaw's (1972) agenda-setting theory was modeled by McQuail and Windahl (1993) in a way that illustrated the theory's basic proposition that "matters given most attention in the media will be perceived as the most important" (p. 105) (Figure 7.4). Like the bars in a histogram chart, the model uses varying lengths of bars to indicate how much attention the media give to different issues and uses varying sizes of the letter X to indicate the importance of different issues to the public. The model brings to mind the idea of measuring differences in both media attention and public perception in terms of relative ranks.

This view of the agenda-setting process, however, has been considerably modified as advancements in agenda-setting theory have been made. For example, it has been found that media attention to obtrusive issues (ones with which the public has direct personal experience) is not as influential on public perception as is media attention to unobtrusive issues (Zucker, 1978). A model incorporating this theoretical development

Figure 7.3   Lasorsa's barriers model of communication, original to this
book

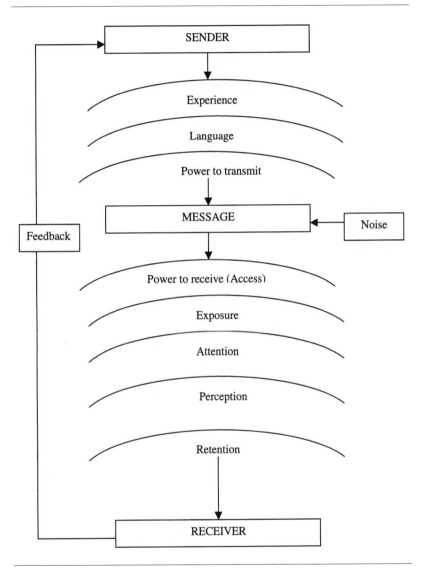

might use distinguishing symbols such as bars made of broken rather
than solid lines or bars of different colors to visualize this difference
between obtrusive and unobtrusive issues. Because size has been used
in the earlier model to represent quantitative differences, the added

Figure 7.4   McQuail and Windahl's (1993, p. 105) model of McCombs and Shaw's (1972) agenda-setting process, redrawn by the authors of this book

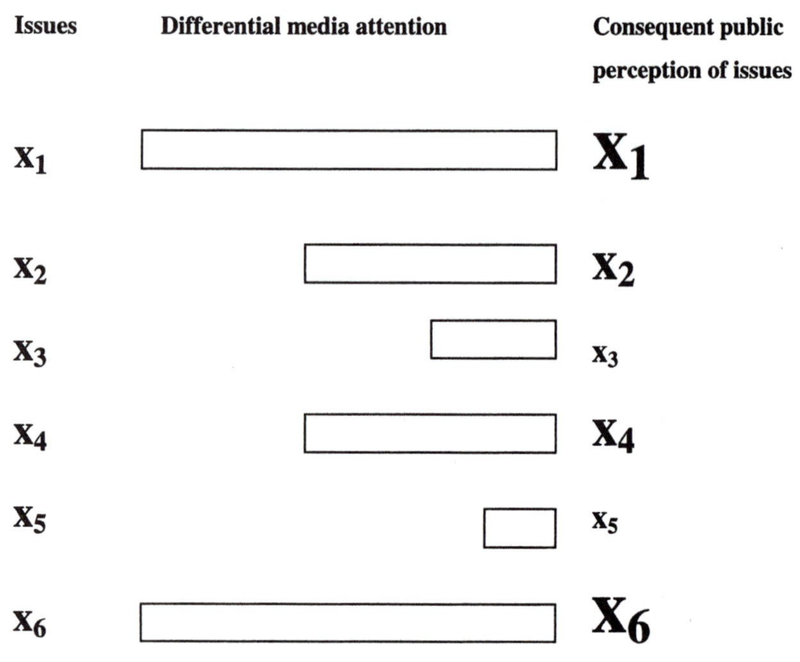

Issues	Differential media attention	Consequent public perception of issues

X_1 ⬚⬚⬚⬚⬚⬚⬚⬚⬚⬚⬚⬚⬚⬚⬚⬚ $\mathbf{X_1}$

X_2 ⬚⬚⬚⬚⬚⬚⬚⬚⬚⬚⬚⬚ $\mathbf{X_2}$

X_3 ⬚⬚⬚⬚⬚ X_3

X_4 ⬚⬚⬚⬚⬚⬚⬚⬚⬚⬚⬚⬚⬚ $\mathbf{X_4}$

X_5 ⬚⬚⬚ X_5

X_6 ⬚⬚⬚⬚⬚⬚⬚⬚⬚⬚⬚⬚⬚⬚⬚⬚⬚ $\mathbf{X_6}$

symbolic representation brings to mind that the difference between obtrusive and unobtrusive issues is regarded not as quantitative but as qualitative. In other words, it is a nominal difference and not one capable of distinction on an ordinal, interval, or ratio scale. A well-constructed model may help us see what kinds of measures are needed and how to design appropriate tests.

Thus, a model can not only suggest that two or more things are related but also indicate how they are related and how we might examine their relationships. The failure of the earliest models of agenda setting to account well for certain empirical findings led to the explorations of the nature of issues that produced the obtrusive-unobtrusive issues distinction. When examining data in terms of McQuail and Windahl's (1993) model, one could see clearly that the theory's expectation that longer bars would be associated with larger Xs did not always obtain. From examination of the nature of the failures, the importance of issue *unobtrusiveness* emerged. That refinement of the model was then tested and found to account better for the findings than did the original model. As Kaplan (1964b) noted, one of the greatest advantages of models is that

> they allow a systematic exploitation of failure. . . . Now models are often used, not in the expectation of immediate success, but in the hope of successive identification of particular causes of failure, so that an acceptable theory can gradually be developed. (p. 274)

❖ CRITICISMS OF MODELS

Though models can help theory builders organize, communicate, brainstorm, and suggest measurements, they do have notable limitations. Sometimes models are criticized because they are so simplistic that they appear to devalue that which they attempt to model. Because humans are almost always elements in social science models, some humanists see all models as demeaning. Further, because models by definition cannot represent all that it means to be human, some regard them not merely as inadequate and unhelpful but as distorting and dangerous because they trivialize human experience (Baran & Davis, 1995, p. 256). Model builders generally respond to such criticism by saying that they can refine models on the basis of research findings.

A second criticism of models is that they tend to concentrate attention on what is most observable and to view these observables as performing most effectively when they serve the overall system. Critics complain that this leads to maintaining a status quo bias (Baran & Davis, 1995, p. 256). The model builder's response to such criticism generally is that not only must the value of each part be assessed in terms of its contribution to the whole, but the entire model must always be grounded in historical reality: that is, placed in the context of its time and place. Take, for example, the case of the standard computer keyboard, which is known as the "Qwerty keyboard" because these are the letters found at the top left of the keyboard configuration. Because the Qwerty keyboard has been used for many years, it might be assumed that it is highly functional. "If it weren't efficient," the reasoning goes, "we wouldn't use it." However, the Qwerty keyboard was actually developed at a time when manual typewriters would jam if keys were pressed too quickly. The Qwerty keyboard was therefore designed to slow down typing, not speed it up. This is why some of the most commonly used letters in typing, such as "e" and "t," are located in relatively hard-to-reach positions, whereas less commonly used letters, such as "j" and "f," are located in the easy-to-reach positions where the fingers normally rest. The Qwerty keyboard was highly functional when it was designed, but today it is less functional. More functional modern keyboards have been designed, keyboards that would make typing faster rather than slower, but people do not like to change, so we stick with the less efficient Qwerty keyboard. In evaluating a model, it is crucial that it be placed in its historical context and that popularity and mere existence not be equated with functionality and efficiency, lest we make the error of mistakenly promoting the status quo.

Related to this is a third criticism of models, that they "can tend to perpetuate some initial questionable, but fundamental, assumptions about the components of a model or the processes at work" (McQuail & Windahl, 1993, p. 3). This, too, critics say, produces a status quo bias, retarding theoretical development. For example, some early models treated communication essentially as a linear and unidirectional process—the movement of a message from a sender to a receiver. Lasswell's (1948) model mentioned earlier is an example of one such model that also has been highly influential. Another highly influential model of the communication process that emerged concurrently with Lasswell's is Shannon and Weaver's (1949). It, too, depicted communication as a one-way process (see Figure 7.5). Lasswell's and Shannon and Weaver's models suited their purposes well, but for other purposes some of the assumptions they make may have lingered well beyond their usefulness. Perhaps this is a criticism more of scholars than of models. When a scholar mindlessly adheres to an inadequate model, then yes, the model will almost certainly retard theoretical development. This is why it is such a bad idea to treat models as revered objects to be worshipped from afar. Models should be poked, prodded, kicked, and torn apart. One of the greatest purposes a model can serve is to be challenged and found wanting.

Other assumptions that models make, however, can be even more general and perhaps even insidious, critics say. As Wallace (1994) noted, "Typically, models are designed to handle routine situations. Assumptions of normality in a situation are inherent in most models. In an unusual or exceptional situation, the model provides no support" (p. 3). Not only can the application of a model in the wrong situation provide no support; it can be downright catastrophic. For example, financial institutions can

Figure 7.5 Shannon and Weaver's model of communication (1949, p. 5)

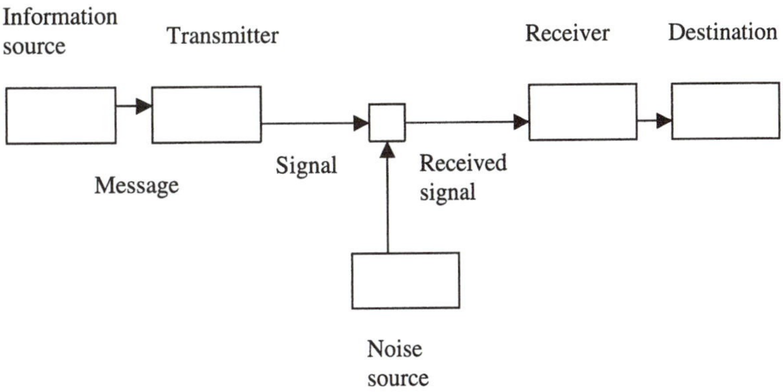

amass amazing amounts of information about potential borrowers and create "profiles" of good credit risks. Slavish reliance on such techniques may make life easier for "model borrowers" but at the same time unfairly discriminate against others whose credit may be fine but whose circumstances are not typical enough to fit the standard model.

A fourth criticism is that models "tend to trap their originators and users within rather limited confines which they then become eager to defend against attack" (McQuail & Windahl, 1993, p. 3). Of course, this criticism can be made about any scientific endeavor, including theoreticians who refuse to let adverse discovery interfere with their cherished theories. One of the strengths of the scientific method is its ability to uncover human willfulness and capriciousness, but we should never forget that scientists are humans and humans tend to tout the familiar and to resist change (Cohen & Nagel, 1934). In many cases, these failings are neither deliberate nor conscious, but the effect nonetheless may be to retard scientific progress. It therefore is a failing against which we ought to be on guard, whether we are building models or using models built by others.

A fifth criticism of models is that they distract us from the primary mission of science, which is to develop definitive causal explanations. Critics say that the identification of powerful causal agents is deemphasized or even ignored in most models. Model builders counter by saying that they can use models to help them suggest predictions and explanations and that as long as model building is viewed as a means to an end and not an end in itself models can serve a useful purpose.

Underlying many of these criticisms runs a current of general dissatisfaction based on the simplicity of models. When scrutinizing a model, one can easily lose sight of the fact that it is simple by design. As McQuail and Windahl (1993) said of models,

> They are inevitably incomplete, oversimplified and involve some concealed assumptions. There is certainly no model that is suitable for all purposes and all levels of analysis and it is important to choose the correct model for the purpose one has in mind. (p. 3)

Severin and Tankard (1997) echoed this idea:

> No one model can "do it all." Even if it could, it would defeat the purpose of a model—a simplified representation of the real world .... If none is available to do the job required, the researcher might well be forced to modify an existing model or even invent a new one. (p. 67)

According to Kress and van Leeuwen (1996), "It is never the 'whole object' but only ever its criterial aspects which are represented" (p. 6), and Holmes and Hundley (1997) referred to a model as "the artifact of choices between what should be included and excluded" (p. 14). If the model builder articulates the criteria used to select the elements and connections included in the model, that can go a long way toward alleviating objections of this sort.

Despite these warnings, scientists often display their models as if, in fact, they do it all. Kaplan (1964b) asserted that the notion that one can construct "a single comprehensive model" of anything "is no more than a prejudice" (p. 288). As he playfully put it, "Models are undeniably beautiful, and a man may justly be proud to be seen in their company. But they may have their hidden vices. The question is, after all, not whether they are good to look at, but whether we can live happily with them" (p. 288).

❖ TYPES OF MODELS

Another challenge facing the student interested in learning how to build and use models is the seemingly bewildering array of model typologies and the different labels attached to what appear to be very similar types, as well as the use of the same label for what appear to be different types. Earlier we alluded to a basic distinction between physical and conceptual models. Physical models, even when they are accurate in scale and precise in detail, offer little beyond simple description. However, we should not belittle such a contribution. Physical models can help us communicate our ideas more clearly, they can serve as heuristic aids, and they can keep us focused on certain elements and connections. They also can be helpful in testing theories.

McQuail and Windahl (1993) made a useful distinction between structural and functional models. Structural models "claim only to describe the structure of a phenomenon" (p. 2). A diagram of a radio receiver and a sketch of a metropolitan daily newsroom are examples of structural models. Functional models, on the other hand, "describe systems in terms of energy, forces and their direction, the relations between parts and the influence of one part on another" (p. 3). Models showing how radio stations or newsrooms operate would be functional. McQuail and Windahl maintain that because communication is in some degree dynamic and involves at least some elements that change states, nearly all models of the communication process are functional rather than structural.

Figure 7.6 is the organization chart of the *Wall Street Journal* as rendered by Shoemaker and Reese (1996, p. 152). It shows the structure of a complex organization in terms of newsroom personnel (boxes) and how they are related (arrows). This "bottom-up" model shows which elements in the system report to which others, from reporters at the bottom of the structure to the company chairman at the top. The model clearly describes the manifest power structure at the newspaper. Notice, for example, that the editorials department is completely separated from the news side, with the heads of both divisions reporting directly to the newspaper publisher.

Figure 7.7 is also a model that describes a news organization, but rather than focusing on the structure of the newsroom it focuses on the functional activities that lead to the production of news. This model, by Ericson, Baranak, and Chan (1987), shows how news story ideas are generated and developed. Ideas can flow from external sources, reporters, and news services. Ideas also can lead *to* sources, reporters, and news services. Once a story idea is identified, it is produced through a series of steps that start with story organization and end with the finished product (content page or anchor script). This model, influenced by Galtung

Figure 7.6   Shoemaker and Reese's (1996, p. 152) model of the organization of the *Wall Street Journal*, redrawn by the authors of this book

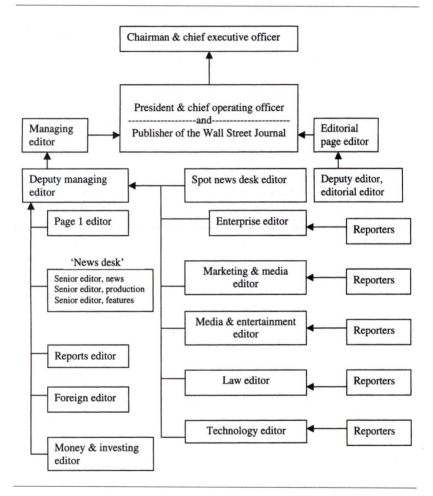

and Ruge's (1965) theory of gatekeeping, shows the classic "winnowing" process through which editorial content is developed. Gatekeepers at various points in the production process let some ideas through while barring others, resulting in what the editor considers to be all the news that is fit to print or, at least, fits (Shoemaker, 1991).

Holmes and Hundley (1997) further categorized conceptual and functional communication models into three types. The "action" model

Figure 7.7   Ericson, Baranak, and Chan's (1987) model of the news
production process, presented by McQuail and Windahl (1993,
p. 179), and redrawn by the authors of this book

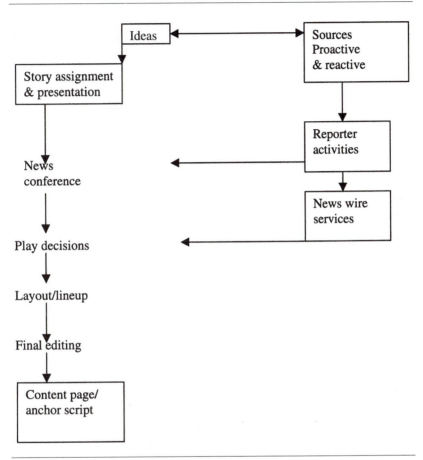

treats communication as "something that one person does to another"
(p. 8). A variety of labels have been applied to such models, including
the "conduit" model, the "injection" model, the "hypodermic needle"
model, the "transmission" model, and the "linear" model. Because
communication in the action model is unidirectional and unilateral, it
resembles what psychologists refer to as the "stimulus-response"
model. An example of an action model of communication is Shannon
and Weaver's (1949) model based on information theory, mentioned
earlier. In this model, the focus is upon the system's capacity to

Figure 7.8   Osgood's (n.d.) model of communication with feedback, presented by Schramm (1954, p. 24), and redrawn by the authors of this book

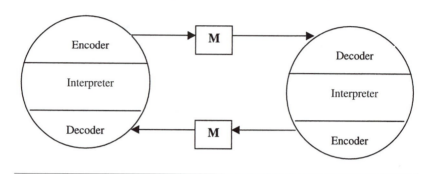

transmit the maximum amount of information successfully—that is, without unacceptable levels of distortion or "noise."

The "interactional" model builds upon the action model through the addition of feedback loops. Because they are more concerned about how humans communicate, Schramm's (1954) early models of communication add feedback as an important element in the process. Such models treat communication "as an alternating exchange of messages" (Holmes & Hundley, 1997, p. 9).

Figure 7.8 is an interactional model of communication originally proposed by Osgood in an unpublished paper and popularized by Schramm (1954, p. 24). Unlike the Shannon and Weaver (1949) model, this one treats message senders and receivers as essentially equivocal, with each party contributing to the sharing of meaning that occurs when communication takes place. Here, both parties encode messages: That is, they put their ideas—their mental images—into symbols they believe the other party will understand. The encoded message (m) is then decoded by the receiver: that is, translated from the symbols back into mental images. The process may be repeated until one or both parties tire of or are prevented from communicating, or both parties feel sufficiently satisfied that further communication is unnecessary.

Holmes and Hundley's (1997) third type of communication model, the "transactional model," was intended to overcome the one-directional nature of action models and the constraints of strictly alternating message exchanges found in interactional models. "The key differences . . . are simultaneity of encoding and decoding and fusing

Figure 7.9   Schramm's (1954, p. 31) model of communication with fields
of experience, adapted by Severin and Tankard (2001, p. 59),
and redrawn by the authors of this book

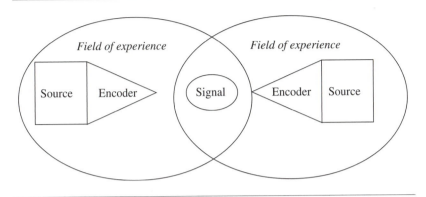

of sending/receiving activities" (p. 10). Berko, Wolvin, and Wolvin's
(1992) model of communication is an example, as are Schramm's (1954)
later models of communication, which include overlapping "fields of
experience" as an important ingredient in the communication process
(Figure 7.9).

The notion of "fields of experience" is important because it
reminds us that efficient communication can take place only to the
extent that the parties involved share certain basic experiences. If two
people do not speak the same language, they may have a hard time
decoding each other's messages. A newsroom that does not reflect
demographically and culturally the diversity of its targeted audience
may communicate poorly with at least some segments of the audience.

Two points are worth making here, one fairly obvious, one not so
obvious. We can see how productive it can be to build upon earlier
models by adding elements and connections ignored previously but
that we now consider important. However, though one might be
tempted to think that the transactional model is "better" than the interactional model, which is "better" than the action model, it is important
to keep in mind the purposes for which the model was designed.
Shannon and Weaver's (1949) simpler model of the communication
process is better at capturing what these model builders were attempting to capture than other models that added components irrelevant to
Shannon and Weaver's concerns. Just because a model is more complicated than another, and just because a model adds something that an

earlier model is lacking, does not mean that it is necessarily an improvement. A model needs to be evaluated in terms of its purposes. As Hanneman (1988) noted, whereas one social scientist may be trying to create time- and space-invariant general laws of social behavior, another may be attempting to uncover and understand the "deep structure" of everyday life (p. 16). Because social scientists theorize about a remarkably diverse range of subjects, we should not be surprised to find an equally remarkable diversity in the kinds of models they employ.

In the study of communication, McQuail (1994) identified four distinct types of models, the first of which he called the "transmission" model. However, what McQuail considered to be a transmission model is not the same as what Holmes and Hundley (1997) meant by the same label. According to McQuail, a transmission model of communication is any model that treats communication as a process of the transmission of a fixed quantity of information—a message—that is determined by a sender or a source. Thus, the removal of unidirectional activity through the addition of feedback and the addition of simultaneous exchanges are not distinctions that make for a new type of model. Therefore, McQuail essentially ignored the distinctions made by Holmes and Hundley and lumped their three types of models together as transmission models. The Westley and MacLean (1957) model, which according to McQuail is perhaps the most complete and most highly regarded early version of a model of mass communication, is thus still a transmission model, even though it contains feedback. Holmes and Hundley (1997), in contrast, would label this an interactional model (Figure 7.10).

Regardless of whether one considers the Westley and MacLean (1957) model to be a transmission model or an interactional one, if we take the time to examine it, we will see what a well-formed and insightful model it is for describing the process of mass communication. First, events (x_s) impinge on a person's (B) senses. Second, some events sensed by a communicator (A) are transmitted to the person, whereas others are not. This communicator is thus the "source" of some information the person receives. Third, some events are sensed by a special type of communicator, a "nonpurposive encoder (C) acting for B," such as a news reporter. Again, C transmits only some messages to the person. Finally, these sentinels (C) also receive information from sources (A), only some of which are transmitted to the person (B). By focusing on the "winnowing" process from the receiver's perspective, the Westley-MacLean

Figure 7.10   Westley and MacLean's (1957) model of communication,
adapted by Severin and Tankard (2001, p. 62), and redrawn by
the authors of this book

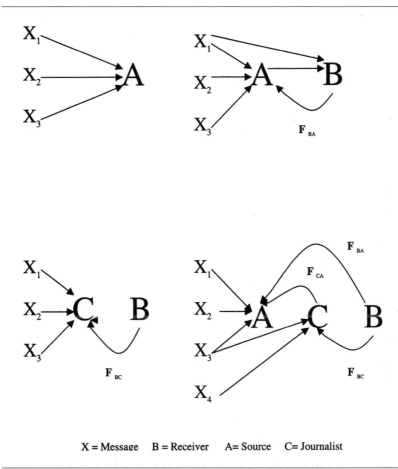

X = Message   B = Receiver   A= Source   C= Journalist

model nicely complements the Ericson et al. (1987) model, which focuses
on the process from the news gatherer's point of view.

At first glance, the Westley and MacLean (1957) model may appear
to be quite intimidating because of its complexity. One of the authors
well remembers when he first encountered this forbidding-looking
model at the start of his graduate studies. After receiving a copy of the
model in class, he turned to one of the other students in the seminar
and whispered, "This looks like Custer's model of communication."

Puzzled, the other student asked, "Custer's model of communication?" to which he replied, "Yes, just look at all those @#$%*& arrows."

Such irreverence notwithstanding, this anecdote points to the problem of attempting to construct a model that, for our purpose, is neither too unrealistically simple nor too inaccessibly complex. Generally, we want our models to be as simple as possible without being too crude. Like Goldilocks in the fairy tale, this may mean going to bed with a number of different versions until we arrive at one that feels just right.

McQuail's (1994) second type of model he called a "ritual" or "expressive" model. According to McQuail:

> Ritual or expressive communication depends on shared under-standings and emotions. It is celebratory, consummatory (an end in itself) and decorative rather than utilitarian. . . . Communication is engaged in for the pleasures of reception as much as for any use-ful purpose. The message of ritual communication is usually latent and ambiguous, depending on associations and symbols which are not chosen by the participants but made available in culture. (p. 51)

McQuail noted that for some media operations, such as news and advertising processes, the transmission model is useful but that for other media activities a ritual model does a better job. Carey (1975) offered a ritual model of communication that focuses on sharing, par-ticipating, and associating. What is considered important in this model is not "the extension of messages in space but the maintenance of society in time; not the act of imparting information but the represen-tation of shared beliefs" (McQuail, 1994, p. 51). Another example is McQuail and Windahl's (1993) "Christmas spruce model of ritual com-munication" (p. 55), which consists simply of the iconic image of a tree decorated for the holidays. "In one culture at least, it symbolizes ideas and values shared and understood albeit vaguely and variously. There is clearly no instrumental purpose" (p. 55). A ritual model of commu-nication also might describe communication that occurs during times of crisis, when the form of communication may be more important than its content and when communication may be distinguished more by its uniformity ("We stand united") than by anything else.

McQuail called his third type of communication model a "publicity" model. McQuail noted that often the primary aim of mass media is neither to transmit particular information nor to unite a public in some expression of culture, belief, or values, but simply to catch and hold people's attention. In doing so, the media attain one direct economic goal, which is to gain audience revenue, and an indirect one, which is to sell audience attention to advertisers. One might say that the primary goal of some forms of communication is to sell eyeballs.

A publicity model can be useful when comparing the performances of different types of media systems, such as commercial television and public broadcasting stations, or national media systems that predominate in the use of one or the other of these types of media systems. For example, the United States has a predominantly commercial-based broadcasting system in which success is measured primarily in terms of audience size, whereas the Netherlands has a predominantly public-based system in which capturing a large audience is relatively less important. This means that in the United States much attention is given to finding efficient ways to grab the audience's attention. However, in the study of news programming formats and content, it is known that factors that increase attention can simultaneously decrease comprehension, and vice versa. Thus, sets of brief stories with dramatic visuals and sounds may draw audience attention but at the cost of greater comprehension. Longer stories with "talking heads" and less vivid pictures and sounds may improve comprehension but at the expense of losing audience attention. This means that media systems that seek to increase attention to their news products may at the same time inadvertently decrease comprehension of their news products. A national media system built upon a publicity model of communication may relegate the importance of audience comprehension behind that of getting a large share of the audience. A comprehensive comparison of attention and comprehension factors in news broadcasts in the United States and the Netherlands shows that these two national broadcasting systems do differ markedly in how they present the news. The publicity model of communication helps show why they differ (Klijn, 1998).

McQuail's fourth model of communication is called a "reception" model. The focus of this model is on the receiver and the power of the audience in giving meaning to messages. In this model, all messages are considered "polysemic": that is, possessing multiple meanings. The context and the culture of the receiver dictate the meaning the message will have. Hall (1980), for example, showed the stages of transformation through which a media message passes on the way from its origins to its reception and finally to its interpretation. Arrows with broken lines can be used to indicate that audience members have the ability to "read between the lines" and can even reverse and subvert the intended direction of the message (Figure 7.11).

This reception model presents unique challenges to the social scientist who must grapple with the many possible readings, including oppositional ones, that an audience can give to a message. For example, an executive of the U.S. automobile giant General Motors once proclaimed that what is good for General Motors is good for the country, a comment that became a catch-phrase in the debate over corporate power in America. This occurred while the company's Chevrolet division was running a long-standing advertising campaign with the slogan "See the U.S.A. in your Chevrolet." Though it appears that few receivers of this advertising slogan saw a connection between it and the other catch-phrase, some did, and the "message" they received encouraged them not to purchase a Chevrolet but to do the very opposite. As McQuail (1994) noted,

> The essence of the "reception approach" is to locate the attribution and construction of meaning (derived from the media) with the receiver. . . . While early effects research recognized the fact of selective perception, this was seen as a limitation on, or a condition of, the transmission model, rather than part of a quite different perspective. (pp. 53-54)

❖ REPRESENTING THEORIES IN MODEL FORM

As models become more complicated (e.g., as they add more parts and connections in an effort to cover more territory or to delve more deeply into territory already covered) and as they become more dynamic (e.g., as they add more moving parts and connections in an effort to show change or the possibility of change), they become more difficult to depict. Holmes and Hundley (1997) reviewed mass communication texts on this point and found that in those that compare the action, interactional, and transactional models of communication, "the transaction model is identified in these textbooks as the best, most complete, and most accurate" (p. 11). At the same time, they said, "The authors of these texts also describe the transactional model as the most difficult to visualize" (p. 11).

Figure 7.11   Hall's (1980) reception model of communication, presented by McQuail and Windahl (1993, p. 147), and redrawn by the authors of this book

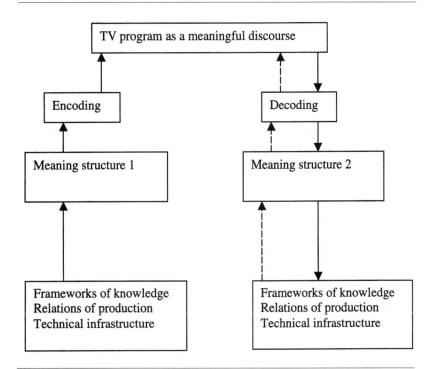

Adler and Towne (1990) suggested that model builders may become dissatisfied with two- and three-dimensional static representations and that "an animated version in which environments, communicators, and messages constantly change would be an even better way of capturing the process" (p. 15). Advancements in computer and communication technologies soon may make such ideas more practical. As Holmes and Hundley (1997) have stated, "Representing a process entails visualizing a story" (p. 12). The crucial point is to have a good story to tell, for then considerable effort may be worth putting into the visualizing of it. On the other hand, as Kaplan (1964b) suggested, a beautiful model may be momentarily distracting, but if underneath the glitter there is not much substance we tire and move on.

Models in the social sciences tend to follow certain general conventions, what Kress and van Leeuwen (1996) called the "grammar of visual design." Holmes and Hundley (1997) noted that although this grammar is incomplete, it reveals "a surprisingly complex set of conventions governing the production of meaning" (p. 19). Models contain objects, which include participants (actors) and goals (actions). The activity engaged in is represented generally as a vector. A vector is simply something that has magnitude and direction. It is commonly represented by a directed line segment whose length represents the magnitude and whose orientation in space represents the direction. Many models indicate vectors as a line with an arrowhead. Lines with arrowheads at both ends indicate bidirectionality. Besides line length, another common way to indicate magnitude is line width. Overlapping of actors or fields that identify actors can imply a vector, as in Schramm's (1954) overlapping "fields of experience" to illustrate shared meaning in some of his communication models.

Vectors in communication models routinely are unidirectional or bidirectional and occur singly or in pairs. The direction and number of the primary message vectors are the key differences among action, interactional, and transactional models of communication. Action models (e.g., Lasswell, 1948) illustrate a one-way vector from sender to receiver, typically using a single vector with one arrowhead. Interactional models (e.g., Osgood's, cited in Schramm, 1954) illustrate a pair of unidirectional, alternating vectors, from sender to receiver and from receiver to sender (feedback response). Transactional models (e.g., Ericson et al., 1987) illustrate simultaneous bidirectionality with arrowheads at both ends of a vector.

❖ DERIVING THEORETICAL STATEMENTS FROM MODELS

As we have seen, a model can help a scientist stay focused by highlighting those parts of a system and the connections among them that the scientist thinks are most relevant and most worthy of study. A model also can help a scientist communicate to others the parts and connections of a system considered most relevant. For the theory builder, a model also can suggest new theoretical statements. It is this last use of models that we discuss here.

As we noted earlier, when a scientist is interested in explaining how something works or in predicting the outcome of a process, he or she often begins simply, perhaps with one independent variable believed to influence one dependent variable. Often, however, the scientist begins to think about how other variables might be involved. As more variables are brought into the picture, the number of possibilities as to how they can be combined greatly increases. For example, if we consider all the possible bivariate combinations with 5 variables, 20 theoretical statements can be derived. With 10 variables, the possible statements increase to 90. (The formula is $(n \times n) - n$.)

Because a model can help suggest relationships, it also can help eliminate them. One powerful technique is to consider the approximate time ordering of the variables. Suppose, for example, that we are interested in how journalists use experts as sources in news stories and that, in particular, we want to know if the gender of the expert is a factor in the frequency of use. Gender is a characteristic that one receives early in life, and for the overwhelming majority of the population it does not change. Therefore, in a study such as this one, it is reasonable to consider gender as a possible cause of other events but not to view it as an effect. Gender therefore would be ordered in time before other variables. In a simple two-dimensional model using the standard visual grammar, gender might appear to the left of other variables. Arrows representing causation might be seen to proceed from gender, but none would proceed into it. By time-ordering the variables in a model, we eliminate from consideration theoretical statements that contradict that order. The result may be what Hage (1972) called a "flow chart of theoretical statements" (p. 56).

Working with a model in this way also may help us recognize subsets of variables that, in effect, represent chains of causes or effects. For example, as we examine our model we may recognize that variables fall into classes or types. We may be able to "bundle" these. Suppose, for example, that we are studying social control in a newsroom. We may be interested in some variables that are outside the newsroom. Other variables may represent newsroom structures, and still others may represent newsroom resources, newsroom outputs, and so forth. We may find not only that variables cluster into classes but that there is a time ordering to these blocks, and it may therefore be possible to establish a unidirectional flow.

Once this has been done, the next step may be to consider feedback. Variables and subsets of variables that move in the opposite direction of the established flow may produce important feedback effects that should not be ignored if one hopes to approximate reality. In the case of social control in the newsroom, for example, the extent to which management hears and addresses the concerns of workers may or may not affect the operation of the system. As Hage (1972) noted of the model-building process, "This may sound like an impossible task, but once variables are written down on a piece of paper or a blackboard, theoretical statements connecting them should quickly come to mind. Finding the variables has always been the harder task" (pp. 57-58).

What we have been describing here is essentially a form of path analysis, using a model as a guide. The product of our analysis—the theoretical statements we derive—will be only as good as the model. If the map is poor, it may lead us into quicksand or over a cliff. To put it in the parlance of computers, "garbage in, garbage out." Computers can easily generate complex path models, but computers cannot easily evaluate them. Scientists may be interested in whether one concept is connected with another, but they usually are interested in more than that. They are interested in causes and consequences.

A productive method for addressing the question of causes and effects is to examine several related case studies. Take a variety of situations from different times and places so that general theoretical statements are derived. Suppose, for example, that we are interested in the role of the mass media in the successful overthrow of national leaders. We might select the Marcos regime in the Philippines, the French Revolution, the Spanish Civil War, Watergate in the United States, the collapse of Czarist Russia or the Soviet Union, and any of a number of other diverse cases that might differ in terms of location, time period, length, violence, and other important variables. The next step is to select these same places at times of relative stability: that is, cases in which the phenomenon exists or predominates and others in which it does not exist or is modest. Thus, we observe the Philippines or France 5 or 100 years earlier or later. We then look for commonalties across the selected cases. We look not only for the presence of factors during times of crisis but for the absence of these same factors during times of stability, and vice versa. How do the media behave across these different times and places? What are the similarities, the differences? Does the role of the media change before, during, and after a coup, and, if so, how? What patterns do we recognize? At this point, some readers might say, "This seems like an awful lot of trouble to go through just to derive interesting theoretical statements." This is true. Constructing productive models and deriving from them interesting theoretical statements is, alas, an awful lot of trouble. On the other hand, building on existing models can be much less daunting and may be a good way to get one's feet wet.

❖ BUILDING ON EXISTING MODELS

Suppose one wants to model cultivation theory (Gerbner & Gross, 1976). This theory holds that television possesses properties that make it an especially powerful influence, such as its relatively high penetration rate (the percentage of the population watching) and saturation rate (the percentage of time people spend watching). Additionally, the theory maintains, the "TV world" varies systematically from the "real world," transmitting constant and consonant moral messages about risk and power. The result, the theory proposes, is that viewers think that the world is scarier than it really is. Thus, for example, heavy viewers have a greater fear of crime.

Because cultivation is a communication process or, more precisely, a mass communication process, we should be able to relate it to any general model of communication, such as the barriers, Shannon and Weaver (1949), or Westley and MacLean (1957) models. However, because any model focuses selectively on a process's elements and connections, we should expect some models to relate better than others to a particular theory.

Consider, for example, how well the Lasswell (1948) model describes the cultivation process. This model begins with a source saying something. It therefore does not focus our attention on important aspects of the cultivation process that deal with why someone says something. At the same time, Lasswell's model draws attention to the channel, whereas cultivation almost ignores channel factors, treating the channel more like a constant than a variable.

Years before Gerbner and Gross (1976) proposed their theory of cultivation, Braddock (1958) suggested that Lasswell's model be expanded to consider two important elements it ignores. He proposed that in addition to Lasswell's five questions to describe an act of communication, two questions be asked: (a) For what purpose? and (b) Under what circumstances? Braddock argued that a fuller understanding of the process of communication results when we consider both the sender's intention in sending a message and the circumstances under which the message is constructed and transmitted.

Braddock's expanded model does a better job of relating to the cultivation process than does Lasswell's (1948) original model. Again, this should not be viewed as a criticism of Lasswell's model; the purpose of his model was not to depict cultivation per se. There is a certain appeal in being able to consider an act of communication as an isolated event.

Nonetheless, there also is a certain appeal to the idea that an act of communication does not really begin with someone saying something but that there are forces at work that lead someone to say something. This latter idea is certainly relevant to the cultivation process, if not to the communication process generally. If we are willing to assume that an act of communication does not occur in a vacuum and that the conditions leading to an utterance are important to consider, then it is possible to expand the Lasswell model in other provocative ways as well. We might, for example, include the idea that reality (the "real world") is viewed through the filter of one's culture (e.g., the "TV world") and that this cultural filtration influences what gets said, or the idea that communication is not linear but cyclical, as in Osgood's model including feedback (cited in Schramm, 1954). If one ignores the italicized terms, Figure 7.12 is an example of a general model of communication that incorporates these ideas. The italicized terms change the figure into a model of the cultivation process. More recent advancements to that theory (e.g., mainstreaming and resonance) could be incorporated into this model as well.

Modifying an existing model to suit one's needs is a tried and true method for advancing science. A review of the models presented here will show the extent to which many have adapted elements of earlier ones. Given that they often are attempting to model the same general process, this should not be surprising. Furthermore, because models are by definition selective, even a slight change tends to have important implications. For example, DeFleur (1970) may have made only one major modification to the Shannon and Weaver (1949) model—adding feedback—but it represented a critical change.

By considering how well existing models represent new theories or theoretical developments, and by modifying these models to create more precise representations, the model builder can help others see more clearly commonalities across theories, how one theory fits into general models, how theoretical advancements make sense in terms of previous models, and other important aspects of theory building.

❖ DEVELOPMENTS IN MODEL BUILDING

Because models are designed to clarify new theories and theoretical hunches, we should expect models to reflect the theoretical interests of the day. Thus, when theories at one time tend to focus upon certain

Figure 7.12   Lasorsa's expanded model of Gerbner and Gross's (1976) cultivation process, original to this book

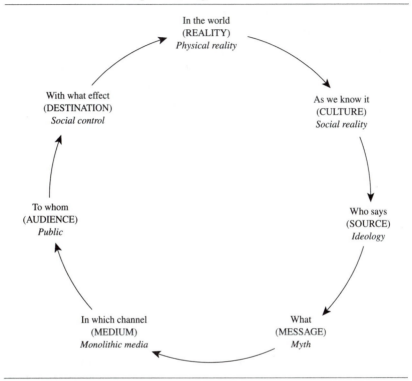

aspects of communication while ignoring others, models should be expected to do the same. For example, when early theories of persuasion (e.g., Hovland, Janus, & Kelley, 1953) tended to focus on inputs and outcomes while treating the mind of the receiver as a "black box," so did the models of that time. Later, when persuasion theories began to focus on such matters as the cognitive processing of information, the sequencing of steps over time (from exposure to yielding), and the varying activity of the receiver, persuasion models began to reflect such interests as well (e.g., McGuire, 1968). More recent theories of persuasion have tended to maintain that humans process information in two distinct ways. When one has the ability and motivation to process, one tends to do so thoughtfully, analytically, and carefully, but when one lacks ability or motivation, one tends to rely instead on peripheral cues and simple heuristics to process information. So-called "dual-process models" of persuasion, such as Petty and Cacioppo's (1981) elaboration likelihood model and Chaiken's (1987) heuristic-systematic model, have gone a long way toward reconciling many of the conflicting findings from earlier research. Dual-process models of persuasion have had two important consequences. They help us see how the same variable (e.g., source credibility) can have different effects on persuasion depending upon whether the variable is a component of an elaborate, systematic processing of information or a simple cue or heuristic ("I yield because I trust the source"). They also point out how attitude change can be enduring, resistant to attack, and predictive of behavior because it results from persuasion through the elaborate, systematic—"central"—processing route or can be relatively ephemeral, easily attacked, and not very predictive of behavior because it results from the cue-based, heuristic-based—"peripheral"—route (Figure 7.13).

Likewise, advancements in information-processing theories such as schema theory have led to new models of perception and cognition (e.g., Axelrod, 1973) that have themselves encouraged the development of more sophisticated information-processing models, such as Graber's (1984) model of news processing. In such models, new information is evaluated in terms of existing schemas (variously called "frames" or "scripts," depending upon the model), which are cognitive structures that codify recurring patterns of experience and make communication efficient. Thus, we have a "restaurant schema" that, when invoked by a message, allows the recipient to focus only on details of the specific message to fill in important details. As long as the sender and receiver both possess a good restaurant script, many routine details can be left out of the message because the script assumes them. We need not mention, for instance, that we ordered food or that we received eating utensils. Communication breaks down when sender and receiver do not share schemas or when a schema's assumptions are violated but not mentioned. Problems also arise when new information violates an existing frame so that the frame has to be modified or discarded. Although that is troublesome, what's worse is when the information, however valuable, is ignored because it does not fit into an existing frame. Processing news thus becomes a matter of fitting information into existing scripts, which are thereby fortified; using information to tweak existing scripts, which are thereby weakened; using information to obliterate a script entirely, which is rare due to its cognitive costs (we have much invested in our scripts); or dismissing the information altogether because it does not jibe well enough with existing scripts. Perhaps the *New York Times* should change its motto to "All the news that's fit to script" (Figure 7.14).

Figure 7.13   Petty and Cacioppo's (1981, p. 264) elaboration likelihood
model of persuasion, redrawn by the authors of this book.

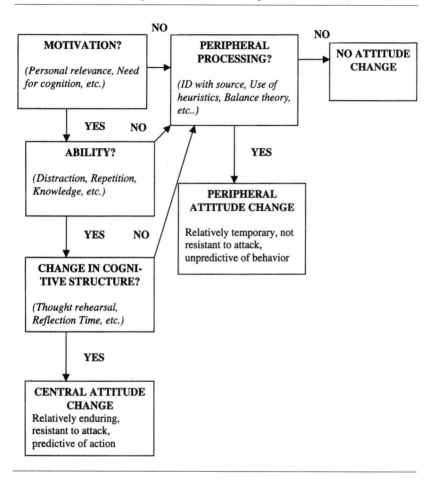

Hanneman (1988) envisioned changes not only in the content
of models but in their form: that is, in the way scientists build models.
These changes in form and content go hand in hand. Hanneman noted
that the observations social scientists make often "are composed
of multiple simultaneous causal processes, operating along multiple
dimensions, and occurring both within and between social actors.
Such processes are inherently complicated" (p. 3). Because of this, he
suggested that more attention be given to dynamics, that models
should use more formal languages, and that greater use be made of

Figure 7.14   Graber's (1984, p. 126) news-processing model based on
schema theory, redrawn by the authors of this book.

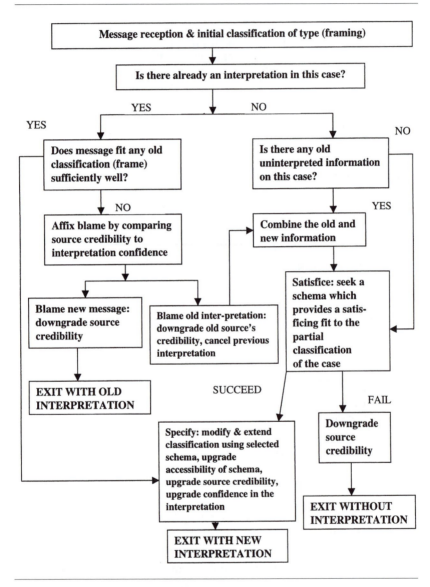

computer-assisted model building and testing. Adoption of these
approaches, Hanneman claimed, would also "bridge major gaps
between those who study 'structures' and those who study 'processes,'

and gaps between those who use 'natural' language to present their theories and those who use formal languages (e.g., mathematics or symbolic logic)" (p. 10). As he said, "The methods of representing patterns of social dynamics in formal models and understanding their implications for computer-assisted experiments have a great deal to offer" (p. 10).

If this were not opportunity enough, Baran and Davis (1995) made the model builder's life even more adventurous by recognizing recent advancements in chaos theory (Prigogine & Stengers, 1984) showing that many important systems, both natural and social, undergo fundamental transformations that cannot be predicted by simply examining past behavior (p. 259). As Gleick (1987) noted, "The traditional models are betrayed. . . . Nature is more complicated" (p. 315). For example, ambiguous messages may be deliberately transmitted precisely because they can serve different functions simultaneously. In many communication models, noise is viewed as undesirable because it is assumed to interfere with the efficiency of the transmission of the message. Shannon and Weaver's (1949) model of communication, for instance, explicitly treats noise this way. Indeed, that model was designed specifically to tackle the problem of minimizing the interference of noise in the telephonic transmission of messages. Shannon worked for AT&T's Bell Labs, and he wanted to pack as many phone call conversations onto a wire as possible without crossover of conversations or other interference. The Shannon and Weaver model viewed noise as a detriment to communication. However, is it always? What of the evasive speaker who is deliberately ambiguous about his or her position on an issue? An effective election campaigner may use unclear rhetoric that may be easily read two or more ways. What of the clever poet who uses words with two or more meanings to evoke multiple images? As Krippendorff (1986) noted, "Noise need not be undesirable as in creative pursuits or in political discourse, in which ambiguity may be intentional" (p. 21). Therefore, models of certain communication processes should be developed in which noise is considered functional rather than disruptive. Examples of the application of chaos theory to social science models also can be found in economics (Arthur, 1990; Grandmont, 1985), political science (Huckfeldt, 1990; Saperstein & Mayer-Kress, 1989), and sociology (Harvey & Reed, 1996; Young, 1991).

There is a bittersweet irony here. As Kiel and Elliott (1996) pointed out:

> Clearly, the fundamental gap between the clear success of knowledge acquisition in the natural sciences versus the rather minimal

successes in understanding the dynamics of the social realm is the inherent nonlinearity, instability, and uncertainty of social systems behavior. . . . Yet chaos theory teaches that the "gap" between the two sciences may have largely been artificial. As natural scientists more intensively investigate complex natural phenomena, they too must contend with the challenges that have long served to keep the social sciences in the position of a scientific stepchild. Chaos theory seems to represent a promising means for a convergence of the sciences that will serve to enhance understanding of both natural and social phenomena. (p. 3)

As both natural and social scientists continue to learn more about the worlds they seek to understand, the models they use will become more varied, more interesting, perhaps more challenging and complex, and, we hope, more useful. Keeping in mind the shortcomings of model building discussed here, we hope further that model builders take to heart the words of Kaplan (1964b), who knew well the value of taking the good wherever he found it: "The dangers are not in working with models, but in working with too few, and those too much alike, and above all, in belittling any efforts to work with anything else. That Euclid alone has looked on beauty bare is a romantic fiction" (p. 293).

Though it is understandable why scientists have been intimidated and confused by building models, it is clear that much can be gained from working with them. If we keep in mind the limitations of models, we may find that by adopting and adapting existing models and by constructing new ones, we may learn much about the objects and processes we study, and we may better convey what we have learned about them to others. Perhaps as a first step we might stop talking about "working with models" and talk instead of "playing with models." Like all the other tools scientists use to gather information and convey it, models shouldn't frighten us. They should be fun.

8

Creativity and
Theory Building

Theory building is typically driven by the desire to explain something. Before there is a theory, there is usually a theoretical problem. But where does the theoretical problem come from? Theoretical problems can come from a desire to accomplish some task, a concern about the social impact or social consequences of something, or a wish to understand some process better.

Theories need to be developed to address these kinds of problems, but where do the theories come from? Theories must be developed by human thinkers. And often this process of thinking in the search for theories is highly creative.

The creative side of theory building has often been neglected in textbooks and classes. This chapter discusses some possible beginning points for theory building and then explores some techniques for constructing theories, focusing particularly on the role of creativity in developing theories and the role of metaphor and analogy in formulating theories. The use of metaphor and analogy is common in theory building. The search for metaphors and analogies is a creative effort that brings a great deal of power to theory building.

❖ BEGINNING POINTS FOR THEORY

The traditional view of scientific research is that it begins with a problem. Dewey argued that productive thinking begins with awareness of some problem or difficulty that provides a stimulus (Beveridge, 1957, p. 72). The frustration at not understanding something can provide a great deal of the intellectual drive that motivates scientists. As theorists, we are trying to find the explanation for some phenomenon. Thomas Kuhn (1970) has argued that all science involves puzzle solving and that the challenge of solving the puzzle is an important part of what drives the researcher on.

The problems that researchers address can be intellectual problems, practical problems, or a combination of both. In the field of mass communication, researchers were at one point struggling with the intellectual problem of figuring out the effects of mass communication. Research up to that point had demonstrated little in the way of effects of mass communication on attitude or behavior (Klapper, 1960). But it did not seem plausible to many observers that mass communication did not have effects. The agenda-setting hypothesis provided one answer to this intellectual problem (McCombs & Shaw, 1977). It suggested that some of the major effects due to the news media are on people's perceptions of the importance of issues or topics and thus are possibly not immediately noticeable.

Researchers are also at times concerned with practical problems such as the possible harmful effects of mass communication on people—particularly young people. One specific version of this question might take the following form: Does television viewing by young people lead to harmful effects? Before society decides to take some kind of action with regard to television violence, we might want to understand the phenomenon better. Concern about the effects of television violence on society could lead a theorist to hypothesizing and theory building about the possible effects. Social scientists have engaged in extensive research to explore the effects of television violence.

Work on building a theory can start with an intellectual problem or a practical problem, but it can also begin in other ways. We can start with a concept we are interested in. Our work on a concept might lead us to think of ways to operationalize or measure it or new ways of defining it. We might also begin to explore the other variables that are related to that concept. It can be fruitful to think of possible causes and possible effects of a concept that we are exploring. This thinking might take us along the path to developing some hypotheses, and at this point we would be taking some major steps forward in the process of theory building.

Our theory building could also start with a hypothesis. Perhaps we have a notion that watching television from an early age causes people to perceive or take in information differently. In exploring this hypothesis, we would probably need to think about some about the different ways that watching television might have an impact on perception and how we could measure these different ways. We might have to invent some new concepts dealing with different ways of perceiving or processing information. One hypothesis could be: "Younger people can process visual information at higher rates than older people."

Theory building can start with a question about something we would like to understand better. For instance, scholars might be (and have been) interested in these questions: How is public opinion formed and changed? How do people make up their mind about whom to vote for in a political election? How are attitudes changed? How do people resist attempts at attitude change?

Another possible beginning point for building theory is to start with an area in which theory is vague or lacking. One example of such an area was the early research on readability. For years, the approach taken by researchers was more or less to put as many variables as possible into a regression equation and see which ones were the best predictors of reading comprehension scores. Perhaps a theory-based approach, aimed at identifying key variables, would have been more productive.

From any of these starting points, we can move into some of the processes involved in building theory. As previous chapters have brought out, when we conceptualize and operationalize variables or begin connecting variables in hypotheses, we are engaged in theory building. *Theory* refers more to a process than to a written-down set of statements. In any research area, a great deal of theory-building work may be going on that is not blessed with the name *theory*. To some extent, theory building is part of the day-to-day research process. Hoffman (1985) stated that "in practice, there is no such thing as a theory, there is only theorizing" (p. 366).

❖ CREATIVITY IN THEORY BUILDING

The important role of creativity in building scientific theories is not always acknowledged. Scientific method is sometimes presented as if it were strictly a matter of logic or a question of following certain specific steps. But many scientists have recognized the role of creativity in scientific research. According to Beveridge (1957), "The great scientist must be regarded as a creative artist" (p. 102). Kaplan (1964a) stated that "arriving at workable theories calls for the exercise of creative imagination, as has been emphasized by countless working scientists, from Einstein on down" (p. 308). Einstein himself once remarked that "imagination is more important than knowledge." Kaplan noted that "we may perhaps speak of 'discovering' laws, but theories must be said to be 'invented' or 'constructed'" (p. 308). Other scientists prefer to leave the role of creativity outside of their description of scientific method. Karl Popper (1959), for instance, said: "The question of how it happens that a new idea occurs . . . whether it is a musical theme, a dramatic conflict, or a scientific theory—may be of great interest to empirical psychology, but it is irrelevant to the logical analysis of scientific knowledge" (p. 31).

In this book, we take the position that creativity is a basic part of the theory-building process and that there are techniques and procedures that can be used to enhance one's creative output. If creativity plays a role in theory building, does that mean theories are created rather than discovered?

Several thinkers, including Kaplan, argue that theories are created. Kaplan (1964a) noted that "a theory must somehow fit God's world, but in an important sense it creates a world of its own" (p. 309). Kaplan suggested that theories have to do with seeing things, not just the way things are: "But the formation of a theory is not just the discovery of a hidden fact; the theory is a way of looking at the facts, of organizing and representing them" (p. 309). He added, "In this perspective, we need not look for the true theory, but countenance and encourage various theories, and without thinking of them only as so many candidates for the single post to be filled" (p. 309). The very notion of building a theory also suggests that it is created rather than discovered.

Several authors have also compared theories to maps, implying that they are tools for guidance in the real world created by human beings. McGuire (1981) suggested that "knowledge is a map" and "theory is a special form of knowledge" (pp. 41-42). To McGuire, theory was like a rope that an adventurous traveler hurls out to cross an abyss. Agnew and Pyke (1978) stated further that "theory-building becomes a game of building models, or pictures of the world" (p. 200).

❖ SOME SUITABLE POINTS FOR CREATIVE THINKING

Principles and techniques of creativity can be applied to the theory-building process at a number of points. The following are some problems in theory building where techniques of creativity could be helpful:

1. Choosing a name for a concept

2. Coming up with new concepts

3. Coming up with possible causes or explanations of a phenomenon or concept

4. Coming up with possible effects or consequences due to a concept or variable

5. Coming up with new hypotheses

6. Coming up with new ways of measuring old concepts

7. Coming up with theoretical rationales for hypotheses

8. Coming up with reasons why a particular bivariate relationship might exist

9. Suggesting third variables to bring into an analysis of a bivariate relationship

10. Suggesting alternative explanations for a result

❖ PRINCIPLES AND TECHNIQUES OF CREATIVE THINKING

The *Oxford English Dictionary* (2003) defines *creativity* as "creative power or faculty; ability to create." By *creativity*, we mean simply the production of new ideas.

Many books have been written dealing with creativity. They suggest numerous techniques for enhancing problem solving and the production of ideas.

Two general principles seem to be important—the suspension of judgment so that new ideas can flow and the generation of as many ideas as possible (Osborn, 1963).

It is useful to think of problem solving or the process of creation as involving two aspects—a generative function and a critical function.

Many writers on creativity stress the importance of first coming up with ideas and later evaluating them. In fact, it is probably impossible to do both at once. Turning off the critical function lets a person do a better job of coming up with ideas. It releases the flow of ideas. But then at a later point it will be necessary to subject the ideas to criticism. As Adams (1979) noted, "If you analyze or judge too early in the problem-solving process, you will reject many ideas" (p. 46). Generating as many ideas as possible also is an important creative principle. Osborn (1963) stressed the idea that "quantity breeds quality" (p. 124) and that our first ideas are often not our best ideas.

Some specific techniques of creativity that might be helpful in building theory are

1. Attribute listing

2. The technique of forced relationships

3. Morphological analysis

4. Brainstorming

5. Coming up with lists of ideas

6. Lateral thinking

7. Random input

8. Setting up provocations

9. The creative hit list

10. Visualization

11. Writing techniques

12. Letting the unconscious do some of the work

Attribute Listing

When using the technique of attribute listing, we list all the various attributes of an object or idea. We then turn our attention to each attribute, using the list of attributes as a checklist to force us to look at all aspects of the problem. Osborn (1963) gave the credit for this technique to Robert P. Crawford (p. 213).

Applying this technique to the field of social psychology or communication, let us assume we are interested in the persuasion process.

We might try to identify the various attributes of a persuasion situation. We might use Lasswell's (1960) set of questions—Who? Says what? To whom? In what channel? With what effect?—to come up with a list of attributes. The attributes might be source, message, audience, channel, and message effect. We then might force ourselves to think about each of these attributes and how it might have an impact on the persuasion process. We might try to identify variables associated with each attribute that might have an impact on persuasion. For instance, thinking about sources might lead us to a variable such as source credibility, and thinking about messages might lead us to variables such as the amount of fear in a message or whether the message presents one side or two sides. This is exactly the approach taken in the 1950s by Carl Hovland and his associates in the Yale Communication Research Program. Their analysis of the persuasion process as involving the communicator, the content of the communication, audience predispositions, and responses is outlined in the introductory chapter to *Communication and Persuasion* (Hovland et al., 1953).

The Technique of Forced Relationships

When using the technique of forced relationships, a creative thinker begins the idea generation process by forcing a relationship between two or more ideas that would normally not be related. Osborn (1963) gave credit for this technique to Charles S. Whiting (p. 213). One procedure for accomplishing this task is to take a list of components or ideas and consider how every idea could be combined with every other idea.

We can again take our stages of the persuasion process as an example. We could take each idea and combine it with each of the other ideas as a technique for identifying possible interactions. For instance, how might source and message interact to produce attitude change? How might source and setting interact to produce attitude change? How might source and channel interact to produce attitude change? And we could go on through the list and examine all other possible combinations. Many of the combinations might not be useful, but the technique could force us to think of combinations that we might not otherwise.

Morphological Analysis

The technique of morphological analysis involves conceiving of two or more independent dimensions of a problem, coming up with a number of attributes for each dimension, and then examining all the combinations. Osborn (1963) gave credit for this technique to Fritz Zwicky and Myron S. Allen (p. 214). It is often useful to put this kind of analysis into the form of a matrix.

One example of applying morphological analysis in the field of mass communication theory might be to come up with a matrix combining elements of the communication process with several theories of mass communication (Figure 8.1). This matrix could lead us to focus on some theoretical areas that we hadn't focused on before, such as the role of the audience in the agenda-setting process. Does agenda setting take place more for some types of people than others? Such an approach might end up combining agenda-setting research and personality-type research, possibly using a personality assessment instrument such as the Meyers-Briggs Type Inventory, a measure of Jung's several personality types.

This matrix might also help us to integrate theories that seem at first glance quite disparate. For instance, we might begin to think about the roles sources play in each of the four theories in the matrix. Are these roles different, or are there some similarities? This kind of thinking could lead to some valuable integration or synthesis of theories.

Brainstorming

Brainstorming is a particular procedure that Osborn (1963) developed to help with group problem solving (p. 151). Brainstorming is done by a small group of people, and it seems to work best with a rather specific problem statement. The basic rules of brainstorming are that criticism of ideas is ruled out, freewheeling is encouraged, quantity is wanted, and combination and improvement are sought.

Brainstorming could have several applications in theory building. It could be a useful approach to coming up with a name for a concept. In 10 minutes, a group might be able to come up with dozens of possible names, and the chances of finding a really strong or appropriate name would be greatly increased.

Brainstorming could also be used to come up with metaphors. We could put a sentence on the blackboard of the form "X is like _____ " and then brainstorm on filling in the blank. For instance, if we were trying to develop a theory dealing with the relationships between reporters and news sources, we might start with the sentence "The relationship between reporters and news sources is like _____ ."

Figure 8.1   Matrix of elements of the communication process by theories
of mass communication

	Agenda Setting	Knowledge Gap	Cultivation Theory	Spiral of Silence
Source				
Message				
Channel				
Setting				
Audience				
Effect				

The various metaphors that were suggested could give us some useful new ways of thinking about reporters and sources.

Generating Lists of Ideas

Osborn (1963) recommended the technique of giving yourself a quota for coming up with a list of new ideas. For instance, in attempting to come up with a title for a new book, one might jot down 50 ideas and then pick the best one.

This technique could be applied to a number of areas of theory building. One example would be in trying to develop the theoretical rationale for a hypothesis. It might be useful to list both as many reasons as you can for why the hypothesis might be true and as many reasons as you can for why the opposite of the hypothesis might be true. This might actually cause you to revise the hypothesis if you could think of more reasons to believe that the opposite of the hypothesis might be true. But even if this does not happen, the exercise should give you some raw material to work into a theoretical rationale.

Lateral Thinking

Edward de Bono (1968) invented the technique of lateral thinking. He made a distinction between vertical thinking and lateral thinking. Vertical thinking takes the most reasonable view of a situation and then proceeds logically and carefully to work it out. Lateral thinking tends to explore all the different ways of looking at something rather than accepting the most promising and proceeding just from that. Some specific techniques for facilitating lateral thinking are random input and setting up provocations.

Random Input

De Bono (1992) suggested using random input as a means of attacking a problem from a new entry point. One way to get random input is to open a dictionary to a random page, put your finger down without looking at the page, and pick the closest noun. The mind will then make connections between the randomly chosen noun and the problem under study. De Bono stated, "It has never happened to me that the random word is too remote" (p. 177).

Setting up Provocations

De Bono (1992) argued that creativity can be spurred by provocative statements, particularly statements that we know to be impossible, contradictory, or logical nonsense. He has invented the word *po* to help introduce such statements. The word *po* indicates that a statement is being used strictly as a provocation. An example of such a statement might be "Po, cars have square wheels." The idea is to make the statement and then see where it takes you.

Examples in the area of mass communication theory might be:

"Po, the mass media do not set the public's agenda of issues."

This statement might lead us to think of situations in which the agenda-setting hypothesis does not hold up.

"Po, television violence is beneficial to young people."

This statement might lead us to question the absolute statement that all violence is harmful. It could lead us to search for variables that cause violence to have more or less harmful effects.

"Po, the public really does trust the news media."

This statement might lead us to look closely at the measures that are being used in surveys that suggest that the public has low levels of trust in the news media. Is the apparent negative evaluation partially a result of the measurement technique?

The *po* word is basically a tool to make us challenge our assumptions.

The Creative Hit List

De Bono (1992) suggested that as part of our creative work we keep a list of problems we need to be working on. He called this list the creative hit list. The problems on the list should be the matters that really need creative attention. The creative hit list has a number of advantages. Just writing a problem down can help to focus it. Putting the problems in a list and referring to the list frequently helps to keep the problems in mind. We can also refer to the list, select a problem that needs solving, and try to apply some of the specific creativity techniques to that particular problem. Finally, we can check problems off once they are solved and move on to others.

Visualization

Many creative thinkers have increased their creative power through visualization, drawing, and sketching diagrams. Adams (1979) recommended visualization as an aid to creative thinking that is "especially useful in solving problems where shapes, forms, or patterns are concerned" (p. 88). Scottish physicist and mathematician James Clerk Maxwell developed the habit of making a mental picture of every problem he dealt with (Beveridge, 1957, p. 76), and visual thinking was apparent in much of his work. A paper he wrote at the age of 14 on the drawing of perfect oval curves was read to the Royal Society of Edinburgh. Maxwell proposed the theory of electromagnetic radiation in 1865. He suggested a hypothetical medium called the ether through which electromagnetic waves traveled. This idea was basically a metaphor, comparing three-dimensional space to a sea through which waves passed. His theory later led to the inventions of the wireless telegraph, radio, television, and radar.

A famous example of scientific discovery using visualization involved the chemist Friedrich August Kekule. He had been attempting to figure out the structure of benzene when he began dozing by the fire. Kekule visualized rows of carbon atoms like snakes and then saw one of the snakes bite its own tail. This gave Kekule the idea for the ring structure of benzene. The idea was a major breakthrough that led to rapid advances in the field of organic chemistry. Kekule's emphasis on visualization and structure may have resulted from his study of architecture before he took up chemistry ("Kekule von Stradonitz," 1998).

Watson and Crick, in their Nobel Prize-winning research that identified the double helix structure of DNA, relied heavily on visualization and on physical models as aids to visualization (Watson, 1968).

Writing Techniques

David Cohen (1977), in his study of how psychologists work, found that many of them got their ideas about psychology while writing. Writing has an obvious utility in getting ideas down before they disappear. But writing can also stimulate ideas. Julia Cameron recommended in her book *The Artist's Way* (1992) that thinkers trying to be more creative get in the habit of writing three pages in longhand every morning. In a similar piece of advice, John Platt (1962) recommended that the scientist spend a half an hour a day writing in a research notebook.

Letting the Unconscious Do Some of the Work

Many authors recommend a technique of thinking hard about a problem and then turning to something else to give the unconscious mind a chance to work. The mathematician Henri Poincaré (1952) had been struggling to prove the existence of a new class of mathematical functions he later called Fuchsian functions. He was trying to figure out the properties of these functions but was having difficulty. He decided to forget about the mathematical work for a while and go on a geological excursion to the country. At the minute his foot hit the step of a bus to take him on his journey, he had a flash of mathematical insight that solved his problem. Poincaré said the appearance of a sudden illumination following a period of long unconscious work on a problem was characteristic of his mathematical work.

Poincaré's experience suggests that one effective approach to problem solving can be to go over a question or problem until it is clearly in mind and then put the problem aside and do something else. Sometimes the unconscious mind will work on the problem and come up with useful solutions.

One important step in applying any of the techniques of creativity to theory building is to give the creative part of the mind the raw material it needs to work with. In most cases, it will be necessary to gather information relevant to the solution of the problem before a problem can be solved. As the saying goes, "Chance favors the prepared mind." It also can help to expose oneself to material from other, unrelated fields. This apparently unrelated information may lead to useful metaphors or unusual ways of looking at the relevant but overly familiar material associated with the problem.

❖ METAPHOR AND ANALOGY IN THEORY BUILDING

One place in the mass communication theory field where we frequently see creativity is in the use of analogies and metaphors. Metaphors can play a useful role by helping us verbalize what is not already in a verbal form. They may therefore be particularly useful in formulating theory, where we are trying to express ideas or insights that have not yet been codified or verbalized.

Metaphors may also play a role in the creative process. They may be close to the nonverbal or visual images that occur at early states of formulation of new ideas. Creative thinking may often begin with images rather than words.

The dictionary defines *metaphor* as "a figure of speech in which a word or phrase literally denoting one kind of object or idea is used in place of another to suggest a likeness or analogy between them" (*Merriam-Webster Dictionary*, 2003). MacCormac (1976) stated that "to use a known linguistic expression to stand for the unknown is the primary characteristic of metaphor" (p. 34). Another scholar noted that metaphors are useful when they bring us "fertility, productivity of new insights and fresh illuminations on old themes and explanatory power" (Aspin, 1984, p. 35). MacCormac (1976) suggested that the fact "that science utilizes metaphors is not accidental, for without them it would be impossible to pose a novel hypothesis intelligently" (p. 10). Gowin (1981) claimed that "the metaphor is the hunting horn of inquiry" (p. 197).

An analogy is an observed similarity between things that are otherwise different. Eisenberg (1992) spoke of an analogy as "an extended metaphor" (p. 144). An analogy is usually more formal than a metaphor.

Use of analogies is a common technique of theory building. It is one of nine techniques for generating hypotheses suggested by McGuire (1976). And, of course, it is a basic technique that McGuire and Papageorgis (1961) used to formulate their theory on resistance to persuasion that became known as inoculation theory.

Miller (1955) suggested that analogy works well when a set of assumptions, definitions, and theorems can be transferred from one class of behaving systems to another. "Newton made a real contribution in developing his laws so that they explained at once the fall of an apple from a tree, the flowing of the tides, and the revolution of the earth, even though these are vastly dissimilar phenomena" (p. 521).

Scientific analogies and metaphors have been shown to serve a remarkable variety of functions, including suggesting new hypotheses and concepts, giving meaning to new theoretical concepts, and suggesting choices between alternative hypotheses or theories (Hoffman, 1985, p. 333). Hoffman argued that "progress on a theoretical level often consists of deliberately exploring the implications of metaphors to expose assumptions or weaknesses and to suggest alternatives" (p. 333). MacCormac (1976) stated that "scientists who wish to formulate new theories that are hypothetical and intelligible almost inevitably must resort to the use of metaphor" (p. 38).

Examples From Mass Communication Theory

Communication theorist Wilbur Schramm was a frequent user of metaphor in his theoretical writings. Schramm wrote of mass communication effects building up over time like a stalagmite on a cave floor (Schramm, 1961), of the press having a "watchman" function (Schramm, 1971), of the child approaching television as if it were "a great and shiny cafeteria" (Schramm, Lyle, & Parker, 1961), and of mass communication serving as a "temperature controlling device" in the process of international development (Schramm, 1964, p. 37).

Harold Lasswell (1960) used a number of metaphors in his classic article analyzing the structure and functions of mass communication. He compared communication in modern society to biological processes, including the operation of the nervous system, and to roles in primitive societies, including those of the watchman and the tribal elder.

Table 8.1 lists a number of metaphors for communication (or journalism) that have been used by mass communication theorists.

Metaphor and analogy have also been used extensively in the formulation of some major theories of mass communication, including agenda setting, the knowledge gap, the spiral of silence, cultivation theory, and news transmission. Below, we discuss these in more detail.

Table 8.1   Some metaphors for aspects of communication (or journalism) that have been used by mass communication theorists. Formulating these kinds of metaphors can be an important step in theory building.

Advocacy role
Agenda setting
Attitude
Boomerang effect
Broadcasting (comes from throwing out seeds)
Bullet theory
Cafeteria line
Canalizing
Channel
Cultivation theory
Decoding
Encoding
Enlightenment
Flow (of news, of information)
Frames and framing
Gap (knowledge)
Gatekeeping
Home page
Hypodermic needle
Inoculation
Invasion (cultural)
J-curve of diffusion
Mainstreaming
Nervous system (communication as a)
Page (on the World Wide Web)
Placement
Position
Positioning
Projection
Psychological warfare
Receiver
S-curve of diffusion
Site (on the World Wide Web)
Sleeper effect
Snowball sampling
Spin
Spiral of silence
Stalagmite
Surveillance
Target (group or population)
Town crier
Traffic
Transmission belt
Transmitter
Watchdog
Watches the horizon for danger
Watchman
Watchman on the hill

Agenda Setting

The agenda-setting hypothesis states that the salience of issues conveyed by the news media influences the salience of issues to the public (McCombs & Shaw, 1977). In other words, the issues that are emphasized in news media coverage tend to become the issues that the public thinks are important.

The hypothesis is based on the metaphor of an agenda at a meeting. One aspect of this particular metaphor is the idea that the person who sets the agenda wields a lot of power by deciding what issues will be discussed. At meetings, items that are not on the agenda typically end up not being discussed. What is on the agenda and what is off the agenda becomes very important in meetings. In the mass communication form of agenda setting, an agenda became a list of issues in an order of priority or importance. The items at the top of the agenda or list are considered to be more important than items lower in the list. This notion led to a method of measuring the lists of prioritized issues, or agendas, for the news media and the public.

Any metaphor has certain connotations. The notion of *setting* in agenda setting carries a suggestion of power and control. The person who controls the agenda of a meeting can determine what will be talked about and what will not and thus has considerable power. By metaphor, this power is extended to the press in the idea of the agenda-setting function. The agenda-setting idea has been a fruitful metaphor that has led to a great deal of subsequent research in the mass communication field.

The Knowledge Gap

The knowledge gap hypothesis states that when information about science or public affairs is introduced into a community or social setting, people of high socioeconomic status will acquire the information at a more rapid rate than people of low socioeconomic status, leading to an increasing gap in knowledge between the two groups (Tichenor et al., 1970).

The knowledge gap hypothesis grew out of an analogy to achievement gaps and economic gaps that were being talked about in society in the late 1960s and early 1970s. More basically, the idea of a *gap* suggests a physical gap or chasm that is difficult to cross or bridge. The notion also implicitly contains the idea of bridging or closing a gap as a desirable goal. This idea of a gap that needs closing probably helped provide some motivation for researchers to investigate the topic of people acquiring information at different rates.

The Spiral of Silence

This theory attempts to explain the formation and alteration of public opinion. The theory applies best to a situation in which supporters of two opposing views are roughly equal in number, but one group judges itself to be in the majority or the group that is likely to prevail (it may make that judgment on the basis of information in the mass media). This group will usually show more enthusiasm or willingness to express its convictions. The other group typically begins to feel left out or ignored and begins to withdraw and fall silent. This restraint makes the view that was receiving vocal support appear to be even stronger. This process continues in a spiral until one view dominates the public scene and the other disappears from public view (Noelle-Neumann, 1993, p. 5).

The spiral of silence is something like a spiral of inflation. The term suggests a process taking place over time, out of control, and feeding on itself or reinforcing itself. The metaphor provides connotations of inevitability and irreversibility.

In her book *The Spiral of Silence*, Noelle-Neumann (1993) used several other metaphors. She discusses the "howling chorus of wolves" to bring out the social nature of human beings, the "storming of the Bastille" to refer to the power of large crowds to shape opinions, and the "pillory" as an example of the power of shame and ridicule.

Inspiring other researchers to think about and explore the ways in which the spiral of silence was like other spirals was probably one of the useful outcomes of selecting this colorful metaphor.

Cultivation Theory

Cultivation theory was developed by George Gerbner and his associates to describe the influence of television in shaping the audience's values and world view. One postulate of the theory, *the mean world hypothesis*, states that people who watch a great deal of television are exposed to a great deal of violent content and that this leads them to see the world as a dangerous place.

The term *cultivation* suggests an agricultural process of growing, of slowly contributing to the growth of something. In the cultivation theory of Gerbner and his associates (Gerbner & Gross, 1976), cultivation seems to be used to some extent as an alternative to causality. Like Schramm's stalagmite metaphor, cultivation suggests a slow process that takes time. This idea of cultivation is helpful in suggesting a more accurate description of the process of gradual change over time due to exposure to television. The concept has the additional benefit of helping to circumvent some methodological problems in demonstrating causality.

This metaphor carried connotations of slowness and gradual buildup that undoubtedly helped researchers to think about the effects of television.

News Transmission

Galtung and Ruge (1965) used an extended metaphor to help develop their theory of international news communication. Their theory likens the world to an enormous set of broadcasting sets, each one transmitting its own signal at its own frequency. This leads to a "cacophony" of world events, only some of which can be attended to. Galtung and Ruge then developed eight implications of this metaphor, each of which became a hypothesis about international news communication. One hypothesis is "The stronger the signal, the greater the amplitude, the more probable that it will be recorded as worth listening to" (p. 261). Galtung and Ruge were flexible in applying the metaphor. For instance, one of their hypotheses is "If the frequency of the signal is outside the dial it will not be recorded" (p. 261). In the metaphor of radio communication, *frequency* would refer to kilocycles, the technical frequency of the radio transmission. But Galtung and Ruge interpreted *frequency* to mean the time span needed for an event to unfold and take on meaning. Thus, in news communication, the building of a dam that takes 2 or 3 years has a long time span in relation to the frequency of publication of a daily newspaper, and the dam might be ignored by the news media because the schedules of the two do not match well.

Advantages of Metaphor and Analogy

These examples, as well as others, suggest that metaphor and analogy can serve a number of functions in the process of theory building:

1. Metaphor or analogy can help us move from a vague notion to a verbal statement or a model. It can help us provide form for the formless. Agenda setting must have started out as a vague notion something like this: "The way news stories are played on the front page has some effect on whether people think the topics of the stories are important." But the idea needed something to give it form, to help it crystallize. The notion of agenda setting served the purpose nicely.

2. Metaphor or analogy can help us generate ideas or hypotheses. Perhaps a phenomenon in one realm has some similarities to a phenomenon in a different realm. It might be worth exploring those similarities, at least intellectually, to see what kinds of hypotheses they can generate. Cohen and Nagel (1934) talked about the difficulty of discovering hypotheses and how analogies can be helpful in doing this. They recommended that researchers concentrate on the facts they are trying to explain and look for resemblances to other facts whose explanations they already know (p. 220). McCombs (1981) noted,

> Metaphoric description encourages creative thinking. In the case of the empirical research on the agenda-setting role of mass communication, the fact that the central concept guiding this research is expressed as a metaphor has encouraged a broad variety of operational definitions and data. (p. 121)

3. Metaphor can help give theory coherence. A metaphor can serve a unifying function. Instead of a set of diverse ideas that are not strongly related, the theory is made up of a group of ideas all related to a central metaphor. The agenda-setting concept has served that function well for an area of communication effects research for 30 years.

4. Metaphors help people to remember a theory. Catchy names aid memory, and metaphors help provide catchy names. A metaphor or analogy can relate the new theory to the already known and can thus make it more memorable, both in general and in specific details. Metaphors can also help in selling or popularizing a theory. Metaphors such as agenda setting, cultivation theory, and the spiral of silence, by being catchy, can help to make theories appealing to an audience.

5. Metaphors can help people to visualize and understand a theory. A metaphor can make a theory more accessible or understandable. Much of McGuire's inoculation theory is immediately clear because we already have some understanding of medical inoculation.

6. Metaphors have a motivational component; they provide a kind of emotional charge or excitement. Hoffman (1985) noted that metaphors "generate a 'tension' or emotional response that drives inquiry" (p. 328). Metaphors can help bring attention to a theory. The metaphor itself might be fascinating. It attracts curiosity that two unrelated phenomena might be related. In addition, the use of metaphor lets various connotations come through that might be appealing to the reader, much like poetry.

Cautions in Using Metaphor and Analogy

Using analogies and metaphors in theory building has some disadvantages as well as advantages. Among the potential drawbacks are the following:

1. Metaphors can be misleading. Different senses of the metaphor might not hold for certain aspects of the phenomenon. The use of metaphor can lead people to see similarities that are not there. For instance, some listeners, upon hearing about the agenda-setting function of the news media for the first time, might assume that the theory is stating that journalists have an agenda, or a set of goals that they are trying to achieve. In addition to not really understanding the theory, these individuals, because of their misunderstanding, might have a negative reaction to the theory.

2. The use of metaphor can lead to imprecise or vague thinking. It may not be clear just what is meant by a particular metaphor. It takes intellectual work to figure out in what ways the metaphor or analogy holds and in what ways it does not. This work may not be done by the researchers. One remedy can be to realize that a metaphor alone is not enough. It should be accompanied by hypotheses or theoretical statements that make the notion explicit and testable.

3. A metaphor can be chosen for its catchiness rather than its accuracy.

4. A metaphor may oversimplify matters. It can focus on one dimension or aspect of a process and ignore others. This can particularly be a problem in the study of communication, an extremely complex, multidimensional process. Metaphor and analogy may work best in the early stages of theory building. Then, through research, the theorist can begin to identify the places where a comparison holds up well and

the places where it doesn't. As a theory grows, these points should be clearly identified. As Miller (1955) noted, "Between any two phenomena there is an analogy and a disanalogy. We hope to develop a theory in which both are recognized" (p. 530). New concepts may need to be brought in to deal with parts of the phenomenon that the analogy doesn't explain. At this point, the name suggested by the analogy may actually start to interfere with theory development. The name may freeze the analogy and make it difficult to change the theory. Miller (1955) cautioned against the overuse of analogies: "Persons eager to advance rapidly our understanding of behavior at times manifest their impatience by hurriedly taking a model from physics or biology and applying it to human behavior. This commonly leads to unjustified oversimplification" (p. 523).

Finding Metaphors and Analogies

Many of the techniques of creativity described early in the chapter might also be used to come up with metaphors and analogies. For instance, brainstorming or random input might be used to come up with metaphors to describe the news reporting process. Such brainstorming might begin with the following stimulus phrase: "News reporting is like _____ ." Then participants in the brainstorming session would come up with words to fill in the blank.

Switching to the Critical Mode

Evaluating Metaphors

It would be too easy to think that all you need to do to produce a useful theory is come up with a metaphor or analogy. Any metaphor or analogy used in formulating a theory still needs to be evaluated in terms of usefulness, aptness, suitability, and so forth. Even a less than perfect metaphor can be a starting point for building a theory, however.

Examining Theoretical Ideas

Once theoretical ideas have been formulated, they must be examined carefully. Theories must correspond to reality. If they are going to be maps, they must be useful and accurate maps. Once ideas have been suggested through the techniques of creativity, they need to be evaluated using the logical, judgmental thought processes. Social psychologist Janet Bavelas (1987), in an extremely useful article on developing research ideas, stressed the connection between empiricism and theory. She described the way a researcher's thinking, even at the conceptualization stage, can change once he or she makes additional observations. The Bavelas approach stresses the importance of a constant interaction between observation and theoretical ideas and the frequent need for reconceptualization in the face of new evidence.

❖ CONCLUSION

Though it is not always viewed as such, theory building is a creative process. It requires logic, careful definitions, and rigorous thinking, but it also calls for creativity in coming up with new theoretical ideas. Becoming familiar with some of the basic techniques of creativity can greatly enhance one's ability to develop theoretical ideas and build new theories.

Metaphors and analogies also play a special role in the formulation and presentation of many theories. Many useful scientific ideas have been expressed in the form of metaphors and analogies. Metaphorical thinking appears to be another fundamental tool of the theory builder.

9

Using and
Evaluating Theory

Theory building is an ongoing process. It doesn't come to an end.
A theory may reach the point where it is useful and can be applied
to solving problems. But it is still subject to revision as further testing
takes place.

Perhaps we should think of theories as moving through stages—
young, middle-aged, and mature. The mature theories are the ones that
have been around awhile, that are more extensive in the development
of concepts and hypotheses, that have been most extensively tested,
and that are possibly being applied to solve the problems from which
they originated.

This chapter begins with a discussion of the weaknesses of atheoretical research and a reiteration of a basic theme of the book, the
importance of theory in research. It continues with a discussion of the
usefulness of theory, a list of ten steps in building a theory, and a presentation of some criteria for evaluating theories. If we can identify
some standards for assessing theories, this should allow us to create
better theories. The chapter concludes by identifying some constraints
on theory building and presenting a few final suggestions that might
lead to better theories.

❖ ATHEORETICAL RESEARCH

Many studies in the social sciences are done without—or with little—reference to theory. Scholarly journals offer a wide variety of descriptive studies. Even some studies attempting to explain do so with little reference to theory. Examples would include studies that insert a haphazard set of predictor variables in a regression analysis with the goal of seeing which ones explain the most variance. These regression studies typically offer prediction without explanation. These kinds of atheoretical research areas have their uses, but they tend to produce isolated studies that do not move our knowledge forward on important questions in the field. As Platt (1964) has noted, such studies become like bricks lying around the brickyard rather than bricks that are used to build a wall.

There may be a number of explanations for researchers conducting studies that are not based on theory:

A. *Expediency.* It is easier to do descriptive research than theoretical research. The formulation of hypotheses that will add to our theoretical understanding is difficult.

B. *Inadequate training.* Thorough training in social science research demands time.

C. *Lack of clear definition or identification of theoretical problems in a particular discipline.* What are we trying to explain? In some fields, the major theoretical problems may be known, and there may be a shared sense of urgency about solving them. Other fields may lack this kind of clarity and focus.

D. *Lack of precedent.* Some areas of research have few examples of good theories. In addition, many social science theories are not well developed.

E. *A field's lack of a clearly defined and agreed-upon paradigm.* Kuhn (1962) has argued that a field moves forward most quickly when researchers identify theoretical puzzles that need to be solved. A shared sense of what the puzzles are defines the paradigm for the field. Many fields may lack this kind of agreement on what the puzzles are.

A major argument presented in this book is that theory-based research is essential if a field is going to advance. Theory has a number of advantages, including that it summarizes knowledge, has practical applications, and helps guide the research process.

❖ THE USEFULNESS OF THEORY

Summarizing Knowledge

A major purpose of theory is to condense and store knowledge. Theories help us to put our discoveries of the nature of the world into statements. Dubin (1978) stated that "the 'need' for theories lies in the human behavior of wanting to impose order on unordered experiences" (p. 6).

The social scientist is interested in discovering general patterns of behavior and expressing them succinctly. This may be done in verbal statements but also through charts, graphs, or mathematical equations. Sometimes a formula, chart, or diagram can express a relationship more precisely than a sentence in the English language.

Practical Applications

Many theories allow people to do things. The goals of science are often stated as understanding, prediction, and control. All three of these outcomes can allow people to accomplish tasks and to bring about desirable outcomes. In the area of television violence, for instance, research indicating that viewing television violence can contribute to aggressive behavior led to the development of the family viewing hour and the television rating system. The National Television Violence Study found that very few violent television programs showed long-term negative consequences of violence and that most violent scenes showed the violence going without punishment (*National Television Violence Study*, 1996). This research could lead to changes in television, with more dramatic programs showing the consequences of violence, more punishment of violence, and so forth.

Guiding Research

A major function of theory is to provide guidance for research. This use for theory comes directly from the cyclical nature of the research process. Where do research hypotheses come from? Often they come from theories. A major contribution of theory is to help guide research. Starting with theory keeps data gathering and observation from becoming a random process or a "fishing expedition." It also forces the researcher to think about the value of a particular research project and how this project will relate to other projects.

❖   TEN STEPS OF BUILDING A THEORY

1. Start with a problem, some unexpected results, an anomaly, an observation of something unusual, something you would like to know the effects of, or something you would like to know the causes of. Bavelas (1987) suggested that the most promising ideas for new research projects often come, not from reading the literature, but from observation.

2. Identify (or formulate) the key concepts involved in the phenomenon of interest (see Chapter 2). Try to come up with concepts that are observable and that can be quantified. This step can be one of the most difficult ones. Often you are trying to identify something and give it a name when no one else has identified it before.

3. On the basis of careful observation and using techniques of creativity (see Chapter 8), try to think of as many causes of the key concepts as you can. These may become important additional concepts in your theory.

4. On the basis of careful observation and using techniques of creativity (see Chapter 8), try to think of as many effects of the key concepts as you can. These may become important additional concepts in your theory.

5. Specify theoretical definitions for all concepts (see Chapter 2).

6. Specify operational definitions for all concepts (see Chapter 2).

7. Link some of the concepts to form hypotheses (see Chapter 4). State each hypothesis in a verbal form. These hypotheses might involve two (see Chapter 3), three (see Chapter 5), or four variables (see Chapter 6), depending on the complexity of the phenomenon and how far along you are in theory building. The hypotheses will often state or imply causal relationships.

Specify the form of the linkage—linear, curvilinear, power curve, or other. Is the relationship bivariate or multivariate? What statistical test will be used to investigate the linkage?

8. Specify the theoretical rationale for the hypotheses (Chapter 4). Why should they be expected to be true? Write this explanation out, either as a paragraph or as a list of reasons.

9. Try to think in terms of multiple hypotheses, as recommended by Chamberlin (1890/1965) and Platt (1964). These multiple hypotheses are sometimes alternative explanations for the same phenomenon. In some cases, called crucial experiments, you will be trying to demonstrate that one hypothesis is true and the other is false. But in other situations, several hypotheses might be supported (lending strength to a theory of multiple causation).

10. Try to put the hypotheses in some kind of organized system. They might take the form of an ordered list. Some hypotheses might be logically derived from others, for instance. Or hypotheses might relate to different parts of a model, such as Lasswell's (1948) verbal model "Who Says What, in Which Channel, To Whom, With What Effect?" Galtung and Ruge (1965) used a metaphor of a radio broadcast station to develop a list of 12 hypotheses about factors that influence international news flow.

❖ EVALUATING THEORIES

Not all theories are created equal. It is important to have a set of criteria for evaluating theories. Authors have listed many criteria for evaluating theories. Some of the most important are the following.

Testability

A theory needs to be testable. Basically, it needs to be stated in terms of concepts or variables that can be measured.

Theorists need to be thinking constantly about how their theories can be tested. For instance, a theorist might have an idea that younger people have a different means of taking in information than older people because the younger group has grown up watching television.

In what ways could this idea be made testable? Part of the task for the theorist in this example would be to try to think of those ways in which the taking in of information might be different.

Falsifiability

Karl Popper (1959) introduced the idea that a theory should be not only testable but also falsifiable. One difficulty in attempting to falsify a theory is that evidence can often be interpreted in a way that supports the theory (p. 107 n.). Popper (1965a) argued that the refutation of any theory is a step forward that takes us nearer to the truth (p. vii).

Stinchcomb (1968) added the idea that a theory must be stated specifically enough that it could be falsified: "That is, a theory to be useful must be specific enough that it might be disproved" (p. 5). Stinchcomb went so far as to argue that "social theorists should prefer to be wrong rather than misunderstood" (p. 6).

Parsimony

The simplest theory is the best. If two or more theories have the same explanatory and predictive power but one is simpler than the other, the simpler one is to be preferred. A theory that is so complex that an individual cannot remember its main points may be suffering from a lack of parsimony.

There are a number of trade-offs in theory building. One is between the simplicity of the theory and the precision of the prediction or explanation. A more elaborate theory will probably allow more precise prediction and better understanding, but it may do so at the cost of being more complex. All in all, the simplest theory that provides the desired level of precision is to be preferred over more complex theories that achieve the same goal.

Some theories of human behavior are undoubtedly too simple. For instance, the notion that the growth in digital communication is going to mean the death of print is probably too simple. Or a theory that stated that all people are influenced equally and in the same ways by television violence would be too simple.

Explanatory Power

The primary goal of theory is to provide explanations. The better the explanation, the better the theory. Likewise, the more phenomena a theory explains, the better the theory. Explanatory power is closely related to parsimony. A theory that can be stated succinctly but can also explain a great deal is high in explanatory power. Another important consideration is that the explanation should be true (Hage, 1972). For instance, we might think that one variable causes another because they are correlated when the relationship is actually spurious. Our explanation will be more correct if we identify that initial relationship as spurious.

Predictive Power

An important goal of science is prediction. Knowledge that allows people to make accurate predictions is important and useful. In general, the more precise the prediction, the better the theory. Interestingly, a theory could be high in predictive power while at the same time low in explanatory power. Dubin (1978, p. 19) noted that in the behavioral sciences understanding and prediction are not often achieved together. For instance, a regression equation with a large number of variables may let us predict some outcome with great accuracy, but we may not understand the mechanisms or processes that are taking place.

Even simple two-variable relationships can have great predictive power. For instance, knowledge of a person's income will often allow one to predict with some accuracy whether the person will vote Democratic or Republican (Table 9.1).

Scope

The more phenomena that a theory helps us understand, the better the theory. A theory that helped us understand the effects of television violence would be more useful than a theory that helped us understand the effects of one particular show such as *The Sopranos*. Hage (1972) suggested that one measure of scope is the number of basic problems of a discipline that are handled by a theory. In the social sciences, most theories deal with a limited range of behaviors and therefore are low in power.

Scope can also be thought of as generality. A theory that is high in scope will apply to a number of different situations.

Cumulative Nature of Science

Theory is not static but is changing and growing. Research is cumulative, with later studies building on earlier studies. Through this

Table 9.1   Relationship between income and party vote in the 1998 congressional election

	Voted for Democrats	Voted for Republicans
Income		
Less than $15,000	62%	35%
$15,000–$29,999	53	44
$30,000–$49,999	51	47
$50,000–$74,999	45	53
$75,000–$99,999	45	53
$100,000 or more	42	56

Data from "A Pitched Battle for the House," USA Today, November 4, 1998, p. 17A.

process, theory is continuously refined as we test hypotheses with appropriate evidence. New studies probe the unanswered questions left by earlier studies. In this way, theories move to a closer approximation to the truth.

In addition, no single study can provide adequate support for a hypothesis. Every study has strengths and weaknesses. It is important to examine a hypothesis with a variety of tests using different methods. Campbell and Fiske (1959) have argued for a multimethodological approach to measuring concepts.

And the progress may not take place without effort and setbacks. As Stephen Jay Gould (1988) noted, "Science is not a linear march to truth but a tortuous road with blind alleys and a rubbernecking delay every mile or two" (p. 17).

Degree of Formal Development

Theories range greatly in their degrees of formal development. We can visualize a continuum of degree of formal development of theories. At the lower end, we would have "areas of research" in which concepts are being developed, hypotheses are being formulated, and data are being gathered, but there is not an effort to be exhaustive about the parts of a theory or to arrange propositions in a logical system. At the higher end, we would have theories made up of systems of propositions, with some logically deduced from others. These more formal theories would also include most or all of the elements of theory discussed

Table 9.2   Sample propositions from general systems theory

1. The amount of information transmitted between points within a system is significantly larger than the amount transmitted across its boundary.
2. Up to a maximum higher than yet obtained in any living system but less than 100%, the larger the percentage of all matter-energy input that it consumes in information processing controlling its various system processes, as opposed to matter-energy processing, the more likely the system is to survive.
3. A system tends to distort information in a direction to make it more likely to elicit rewards or less likely to elicit punishments to itself.
4. A system gives priority processing to information that will relieve a strain (i.e., that it "needs"), neglecting neutral information. It positively rejects information that will increase a strain.
5. A system usually associates with other systems that have arisen from similar templates rather than with those derived from dissimilar templates.

SOURCE: Miller (1995, pp. 92, 93, 94, 95, 114).

in this book—concepts, theoretical definitions, operational definitions, hypotheses, theoretical linkages, operational linkages, limits, and assumptions. Some theories in the social sciences, such as Miller's (1955, 1995) general system theory, are at the higher end of the scale (Table 9.2). Many areas of research in the communication field appear to be at the lower end.

When we are thinking about the degree of formality of a theory, it is useful to examine how authors present their own work. Is it presented as a formal theory? Is it called a theory? When should an area (or hypothesis) be called a theory? Maybe some good theoretical work is going on in an area to which the label *theory* has not yet been applied. Most of our theories in the social sciences are not finished—they are works in progress. Many of them are in early stages of development. They may not be written down in one place as completed theories, but they may have many of the components that we have presented in this book—concepts, theoretical statements, theoretical rationales, theoretical and operational definitions, and so forth.

Social science theories often consist of verbal statements or hypotheses. It may be desirable to move to a more formal, mathematical form for these theories. Often theories that consist of verbal statements can be recast as path models. A path model can be created by identifying the variables and representing them as boxes, then specifying the linkages between them with lines or arrows (see Chapter 7 for a discussion of path models).

Heuristic Value

A theory is valuable when it helps us generate ideas for research and when it leads to other theoretical ideas. The more new hypotheses that can be generated from a theory, the better the theory.

Aesthetics

Although it is perhaps not an essential criterion, some writers suggest applying an aesthetic principle to the evaluation of theories. Kaplan (1964, p. 318) claimed that a theory can be beautiful. In a similar way of thinking, physicists sometimes talk about an idea or explanation being "sweet."

Unfortunately, it is likely that all these criteria cannot be fulfilled simultaneously. For instance, there is probably a trade-off between generality, simplicity, and accuracy. "It is impossible for an explanation of social behavior to be simultaneously general, simple, and accurate" (Thorngate, 1976, p. 126).

The parts of a theory presented in this book—concepts, theoretical definitions, operational definitions, hypotheses, theoretical linkages, operational linkages, limits, and assumptions—give us one more way of evaluating a theory. How many of the parts have been developed, and how well have they been developed? The more parts have been explicitly dealt with and included, the better the theory.

Other discussions of criteria for evaluating theories can be found in Hage (1972), Agnew and Pyke (1978), Littlejohn (1983), and Burgoon and Buller (1996).

❖ SAMPLE EVALUATION OF A THEORY

It may help the reader to understand the 10 criteria for evaluating a theory if they are applied to a particular theory. In the following paragraph and Table 9.3, the 10 criteria are applied to cultivation theory, a theory developed by George Gerbner and his associates (Gerbner, Gross, Morgan, & Signorielli, 1986, 1994) to explain the effects of

Table 9.3   An evaluation of cultivation theory

Criterion	Rating
1. Testability	Moderate

Key variables are measurable, but the hypothesized long-term effect can be difficult to detect.

2. Falsifiability   Moderate
Results not supporting the hypothesis have typically led to reformulation of the theory rather than falsification.

3. Parsimony   High
The theory started with one basic hypothesis. Revisions have added the ideas of resonance and mainstreaming, and the effects have been split into first order and second order. But the theory is still limited to a few concepts and hypotheses.

4. Explanatory power   Low
When other variables are controlled for, the amount of variation explained by television viewing becomes rather small. The suggestion by some researchers that cultivation effects are genre or program specific reduces the power of the theory quite a bit.

5. Predictive power   Low
The relatively low correlations that are typically found make it difficult to predict effects on viewers with precision.

6. Scope   High
One reason this theory is appealing is that it describes the effects of television viewing, and television is the most popular mass medium. The theory also deals with how people's values and worldviews are shaped—another area of wide applicability.

7. Cumulative nature of research and theory   Moderate
Cultivation theory has been one of the most popular theories in the mass communication field, and there has been extensive research on the topic over a 30-year period. The theory has been revised a number of times on the basis of research evidence. It shows cumulative growth better than many other areas. But there has also been some resistance to changing the original formulation of the theory.

8. Degree of formal development   Moderate
Much has been written about cultivation theory, and many of the elements of a formal theory have been presented. But the emphasis has been on reporting empirical research findings rather than spelling out the theory. The theory has been reported in a series of journal articles and has not been pulled together in a formal presentation.

9. Heuristic value   High
The theory has generated a great deal of research in the 30-plus years since it was first presented.

10. Aesthetics   Low
The original idea was beautiful in its simplicity and truthfulness. Additions of later concepts such as mainstreaming and resonance have made it more cumbersome. The idea that cultivation effects are genre specific reduces the sweep of the theory and makes it more mundane.

television watching on viewers' values and worldviews. This theory initially presented one main hypothesis, which stated that watching television shapes viewers' beliefs, ideologies, and worldviews. The hypothesis was modified later in the face of research evidence indicating that cultivation effects did not hold up across the board for all viewers.

The revised cultivation hypothesis introduced the concepts of *mainstreaming* and *resonance.* These concepts specified the conditions under which cultivation would be more or less likely to occur. But the added concepts may have also limited the scope and explanatory power of the theory. Some writers have also suggested that the revised theory incorporating mainstreaming and cultivation allows for so many outcomes that it has rendered the theory unfalsifiable.

Scholars have also debated whether the hypothesis in its original form, which looked at television viewing as the major independent variable, is too general. Researchers have suggested that cultivation effects may differ depending on the kind of television program being watched—that is, cultivation effects may be *program specific.* Further revisions of the theory have separated the effects into two types—first-order beliefs (reality-based perceptions, such as rate of occurrence of a particular crime) and second-order beliefs (for instance, the idea that the world is a dangerous place).

Although cultivation theory has been one of the most active areas of communication research, it still seems to be an area of research more than a theory. It is difficult to say whether it is an area showing a healthy cumulative growth and refinement of hypotheses or an area in trouble because some of the main propositions have not been supported by evidence and the scope of the theory is being diminished by the new propositions.

❖ THEORY BUILDING AND PLATT'S "STRONG INFERENCE"

Platt (1964) noted some time ago that certain areas of science, including molecular biology, have moved forward much more rapidly than others. He suggested that this rapid progress has occurred because these areas have used a particularly effective approach to research that he called *strong inference.*

Strong inference is a specific way of thinking about research. The method involves suggesting multiple hypotheses, subjecting the hypotheses to tests that permit sharp exclusion of certain hypotheses, and then formulating new multiple hypotheses to move the process forward another step. The process allows research to progress along logical branches, with certain branches being eliminated because they are not supported by evidence. Then the process moves to the next branching point.

Strong inference and falsifiability of hypotheses seem to go together well. Hypotheses and theories that are capable of falsification will allow the sharp exclusion of wrong hypotheses that is required by strong inference thinking. Strong inference implies a linear progress in research that may be difficult to achieve in the social sciences but is still worth striving for.

❖ CONSTRAINTS ON THEORY BUILDING

Several forces, some obvious and some not so obvious, act to constrain the building of theory. Four of the most important are listed here.

1. Availability of funding causes some theoretical problems to receive a great deal of attention from researchers and others to be ignored (Martin, 1982, p. 27). In the mass communication research field, funding has frequently been made available for research on the effects of television violence. As a consequence, researchers who might have studied other theoretical problems ended up conducting studies of television violence.

2. There are constraints on the operationalizations of variables, or the choices of measurements (Kulka, 1982, p. 58). A familiar example is the secondary analysis of survey data, where the researcher is forced to use questions developed by other researchers for other purposes. Researchers are also constrained by their tendency to use the operationalizations of variables that have been used by prior researchers. Even beyond these considerations, if something is not easy to measure, it is less likely to be studied. "Much of what is considered an acceptable area of investigation is that for which there exists the possibility of operationalization" (DeCarufel, 1976, pp. 336-337).

3. Choices must be made in the formulation of theory. One choice has to do with the scope or generalizability of the theory. It might be possible to create a theory that would allow nearly perfect prediction

of a very specific phenomenon. Such a theory might actually be close to a simulation. This would be a theory that was deliberately narrow in scope. Or the theorist might choose to go in the other direction and create a theory that would explain a much larger class of phenomena, such as a theory of aggressive behavior. McGrath (1982) pointed out that a theory that is high in generalizability will probably be low in realism of context and in precision of measurement. This might be called the "precision versus scope dilemma" (p. 93).

4. Certain statistical models direct researchers toward certain kinds of problems. For instance, many researchers think in terms of statistical tests, and a common approach in statistics is to try to explain as much variance as possible. But this way of looking at research may lead the theorist to ignore problems that do not involve variation. For instance, much of the content of the mass media may be similar from day to day. How could a researcher investigate the effects of this similarity? "The pursuit of variance leads researchers to pick certain problems and ignore others" (Lieberson, 1985, p. 91). The "explaining the variance" approach has other limitations. It implies that causes are being found, when in fact the relationships being uncovered are often rather weak. For instance, a study that yields a correlation (or a multiple correlation) of .40 is explaining only 16% of the variance. What about the other 84%?

❖ FINAL SUGGESTIONS

The following suggestions should lead to better theory building:

1. Be aware of the various constraints on theory building, and try to minimize their impact.

2. Operationalize variables so that they have a number of points on a continuum, not just two.

3. In testing propositions, use multiple methods (see Campbell & Fiske, 1959).

4. Be wary of the *explaining the variance* approach. It has its uses, but it also has its limitations. One alternative is the process of exclusion of possible explanations advocated in the *strong inference* approach.

5. Be prepared for failure and ready to move on anyway. Darwin and Faraday said that most hypotheses turn out to be wrong (Beveridge, 1957, p. 79). Campbell and Stanley (1963) said we should inoculate graduate students to expect failure in testing hypotheses. Beveridge (1957, p. 97) said that not all intuitions turn out to be correct.

6. Editors of journals and reviewers of manuscripts should look for contributions to theory in the manuscripts they review and be more willing to publish manuscripts that are aimed at theory building.

❖ CONCLUSION

Many of the social sciences may be held back by a lack of attention to theory building. Much research has shown an overemphasis on collection of empirical data without a clear sense of theoretical purpose. One of the easiest ways many researchers could improve their research would be through increased attention to theory building. The payoff for the individual researcher and the field overall would be more efficient summarization of information and a clearer sense of direction about future research.

Appendix A

❖ GUIDELINES FOR PREPARING TABLES AND FIGURES

Before you collect data for any quantitative research project, you should think carefully about the kind of statistical analyses you'll need to test your hypotheses. Before collecting any data, we recommend preparing preliminary tables and figures to show all analyses necessary to test the hypotheses. Of course, this does not preclude post hoc analysis (correctly identified as such), but it ensures that you will have all of the data you need and that you will understand what you're about to do.

Attached are some examples of using various statistics. These are not presented as the only way to show statistics, but they are straightforward and easy to read.

1. *Univariate (descriptive) statistics*—You should provide one or more tables with a univariate statistic for every variable used in your study. Variables that are measured at interval or ratio levels can be adequately described with means and standard deviations, and many of these can be presented in one table. Variables that are measured at nominal or ordinal levels should be presented as percentages ("valid" percentages, that is, with missing data removed). You may be able to group several "percentage" variables on one table, or you may need to present one per table. Be sure to give an N for each variable, whether nominal/ordinal or interval/ratio.

2. *Bivariate (inferential) statistics*—This is your first run at testing your hypotheses, but if you have some "control" variables (we encourage you to use them), you will probably also want to look at the bivariate relationships between your control variables and the independent and dependent variables. For interval/ratio variables,

this will probably mean a correlation analysis, such as Pearson's r. For ordinal variables, use Kendall's tau, unless you are using rank-order data; then use Spearman's rho. (Table formats for Pearson's r, Kendall's tau, and Spearman's rho are all the same. Hence, only Pearson's r is shown in the following examples.) For nominal variables, use chi-square and either phi or Cramer's V (phi for a 2×2 table, Cramer's V for all other tables). Chi-square tells you whether the two concepts are related; phi and V tell you how strong the relationship is.

3. *Multivariate (inferential) statistics*—One of the steps involved in establishing a causal relationship in research is ruling out alternative explanations for the bivariate relationships observed. This is done by statistically controlling for third (and fourth, etc.) variables. For relationships between nominal and ordinal variables, this will probably be cross-tabulation with a control variable (and either the chi-square/ phi/Cramer's V combination or Kendall's tau to test the original rela-tionship within each category of the control variable). For interval and ratio variables, this will probably be partial r or hierarchical regression analysis. For a good analysis of three-variable relationships, see Chapter 5 of this book. It is generally more useful to show three-variable rela-tionships in figure form, but both the table and figure formats are shown here.

❖ BLANK TABLE GUIDELINES

Although there are as many ways to present research products as there are researchers, the following have served us (and our students) well in the past. Some journals have different styles, and researchers should always follow their field's protocols.

1. We prefer that you indicate the level of statistical significance as either $p < .05$, $p < .01$, $p < .001$, or *ns* (not significant). Presenting the exact probability estimates given by a statistical program implies more precision of estimates than we can really have, based on our imprecise operational definitions.

2. Statistics are generally rounded to two decimal places. Do not use leading zeros (e.g., 0.45 should be .45). Use a format that will align numbers in a column along the decimal point.

3. We believe that the operational definitions for all variables in the tables should be presented as footnotes. This aids in interpretation of the statistics: for example, whether a Likert scale uses 1 or 5 for *strongly disagree*. Interpreting a mean of 4.25 will depend on the information. Any statistics based on correlations will also need operational definition information to interpret. The object is for a table to be interpretable on its own, without reference to the text.

4. We've replaced the real numbers with N's: nn.n. You can omit these in the tables you prepare before you collect your data. Just leave the spaces blank.

Tables That Present Descriptive Statistics
Table 1. Means and standard deviations for interval- or ratio-level variables
Table 2. Percentages for nominal- or ordinal-level variables

Tables That Present Bivariate Statistics
Table 3. Cross-tabulation of a nominal variable by a nominal variable*
Table 4. Independent tests for interval- or ratio-level variables by a dichotomous variable consisting of independent groups of cases
Table 5. Correlated t tests for interval- or ratio-level variables using the same scale
Table 6. One-way analysis of variance for interval- or ratio-level variables by one categorical variable, with means and standard deviations
Table 7. Pearson correlation coefficients for interval- and ratio-level variables**

Tables That Present Multivariate Statistics
Table 8. Cross-tabulation with one control variable
Table 9. Two-way analysis of variance
Figure 1. Two-way analysis of variance
Table 10. Analysis of covariance
Table 11. Partial correlation coefficients
Table 12. Multiple regression analysis
Table 13. Factor analysis

* Or nominal by ordinal (or vice versa) or ordinal by ordinal.
** This same format can be used for matrices producing other correlation coefficients, including Kendall's tau (for ordinal variables) and Spearman's rho (for rank-order variables).

Table 1   Means and standard deviations for media use, likelihood to vote, election knowledge, and demographic variables

Variables	Mean	SD	N
On the average, how many days a week do you read a daily newspaper?*	n.nn	n.nn	nnn
On the average, how many days a week do you watch local TV news?*	n.nn	n.nn	nnn
On the average, how many days a week do you watch national TV news?*	n.nn	n.nn	nnn
It is important for me to have a daily newspaper to read in Spanish**	n.nn	n.nn	nnn
It is important for me to have access to a local TV newscast in Spanish**	n.nn	n.nn	nnn
I plan to vote in the upcoming election for U.S. president**	n.nn	n.nn	nnn
Knowledge about election***	nn.nn	n.nn	nnn
Age (in years)	nn.nn	nn.nn	nnn
Education (in years)	nn.nn	nn.nn	nnn
Income****	n.nn	n.nn	nnn

*Responses were coded from 0 to 7 days a week.

**Responses were coded 5 = *strongly agree*, 4 = *agree*, 3 = *neutral*, 2 = *disagree*, 1 = *strongly disagree*.

***Number of correct answers, ranging from 0 to 10.

****1 = $10,000 or under; 2 = $20,000 to 29,999; 3 = $30,000 to 39,999; 4 = $40,000 to 49,999; 5 = $50,000 to 59,999; 6 = $60,000 to 69,999; 7 = $70,000 to 79,999; 8 = $80,000 to 80,999; 9 = $90,000 or more.

Table 2   Percentages for gender and media reliance variables

Variables	%
Gender	
Male	nn.nn
Female	nn.nn
	100.00%
	(N = nnn)
From which of the following do you get most of your news and public affairs information?	
Newspapers	nn.nn
Television	nn.nn
Magazines	nn.nn
Radio	nn.nn
People	nn.nn
	100.00%
How good a job is George W. Bush doing as U.S. president?	
Very good	nn.nn
Good	nn.nn
Fair	nn.nn
Poor	nn.nn
	100.00%
	(N = nnn)
Did you vote in the 2004 election for U.S. president?	
Yes	nn.nn
No	nn.nn
	100.00%
	(N = nnn)

Table 3   Cross-tabulation of main source of news and public affairs information by respondent's gender

From which of the following do you get most of your news and public affairs information?	*Respondent's gender*	
	Male	*Female*
Newspapers	nn.n %	nn.n %
Television	nn.n	nn.n
Magazines	nn.n	nn.n
Radio	nn.n	nn.n
People	nn.n	nn.n
	100.0%	100.0%
	(N = nnn)	(N = nnn)

If one or both variables are measured at the nominal level, use chi-square and Cramer's V or phi:

X^2 = nn.nn, df = n, $p <$ .nn (or *ns*)

Cramer's V (or phi) = .nn

If both variables are measured at least at the ordinal level, use Kendall's tau b or tau c (tau b is for tables where the number of rows equals the number of columns; tau c for other tables):

Kendall's tau b (or c) = .nn , $p <$ .nn (or *ns*)

Note: The independent variable should be the column variable, and the dependent variable should be the row variable.

Table 4   Independent *t* tests for media use variables by respondent's gender

Variables	Male mean (& SD) (N = nnn)	Female mean (& SD) (N = nnn)	t value	df	Significance
On the average, how many days a week do you read a daily newspaper?*	n.nn (n.nn)	n.nn (n.nn)	n.nn	nnn	$p < .nn$ (or ns)
On the average, how many days a week do you watch local television news?*	n.nn (n.nn)	n.nn (n.nn)	n.nn	nnn	$p < .nn$ (or ns)
On the average, how many days a week do you watch national television news?*	n.nn (n.nn)	n.nn (n.nn)	n.nn	nnn	$p < .nn$ (or ns)
It is important for me to have a daily newspaper to read in Spanish.**	n.nn (n.nn)	n.nn (n.nn)	n.nn	nnn	$p < .nn$ (or ns)
It is important for me to have access to a local TV newscast in Spanish.**	n.nn (n.nn)	n.nn (n.nn)	n.nn	nnn	$p < .nn$ (or ns)
General importance of Spanish news.***	n.nn (n.nn)	n.nn (n.nn)	n.nn	nnn	$p < .nn$ (or ns)

*Responses were coded 0 to 7 days a week.
**Responses were coded: 5 = *strongly agree*, 4 = *agree*, 3 = *neutral*, 2 = *disagree*, 1 = *strongly disagree*.
***Additive index of the two previous variables, ranging from 10 (strongly agree) to 2 (strongly disagree). Cronbach's alpha = n.nn.

Table 5   Correlated t tests for media use variables

Variables	Mean	SD	t value	df	Significance
On the average, how many days a week do you read a daily newspaper?*	n.nn	nn.nn			
On the average, how many days a week do you watch local TV news?*	n.nn	nn.nn	n.nn	nnn	$p <$ .nn (or *ns*)
On the average, how many days a week do you read a daily newspaper?*	n.nn	nn.nn			
On the average, how many days a week do you watch national TV news?*	n.nn	nn.nn	n.nn	nnn	$p <$ .nn (or *ns*)
On the average, how many days a week do you watch local TV news?*	n.nn	nn.nn			
On the average, how many days a week do you watch national TV news?*	n.nn	nn.nn	n.nn	nnn	$p <$ .nn (or *ns*)

* Responses were coded 0 to 7 days per week.

Table 6   One-way analyses of variance for election knowledge and
likelihood of voting by media reliance

| Variables | *Media reliance* | | | | | |
	Newspaper mean (SD)	*Television mean (SD)*	*Radio mean (SD)*	*F*	*df*	*Significance*
Election knowledge*	n.nn (n.nn)	n.nn (n.nn)	n.nn (n.nn)	n.nn	n.nn	$p < .nn$ (or ns)
I will vote in the upcoming election for U.S. president**	n.nn (n.nn)	n.nn (n.nn)	n.nn (n.nn)	n.nn	n.nn	$p < .nn$ (or ns)

* Responses were coded from 0 to 7 days a week.
** Responses were coded 5 = *strongly agree,* 4 = *agree,* 3 = *neutral,* 2 = *disagree,* 1 = *strongly disagree.*

Table 7   Pearson correlation coefficients for media use and election variables

Variables	2	3	4	5	6	7
1. Newspaper exposure*	.nn[a] (nnn)	.nn (nnn)	.nn[b] (nnn)	.nn (nnn)	.nn (nnn)	.nn[c] (nnn)
2. Local TV news exposure*	—	.nn (nnn)	.nn[b] (nnn)	.nn (nnn)	.nn (nnn)	.nn[c] (nnn)
3. National TV news exposure*		—	.nn[b] (nnn)	.nn (nnn)	.nn (nnn)	.nn[c] (nnn)
4. Importance of Spanish-language newspaper**			—	.nn[b] (nnn)	.nn (nnn)	.nn (nnn)
5. Importance of Spanish-language local TV news**				—	.nn (nnn)	.nn[c] (nnn)
6. Election knowledge***					—	.nn[c] (nnn)
7. Likelihood of voting**						—

* Responses were coded from 0 to 7 days a week.

**Responses were coded 5 = *strongly agree*, 4 = *agree*, 3 = *neutral*, 2 = *disagree*, 1 = *strongly disagree*.

***Number of correct answers, ranging from 0 to 10.

a. $p < .05$.

b. $p < .01$.

c. $p < .001$.

Table 8   Cross-tabulation of main source of news and public affairs information by respondent's gender, controlling for whether the person voted in the 2000 election for U.S. president*

From which of the following do you get most of your news and public affairs information?	(No controls) Gender		Did you vote in the 2004 election for U.S. president? Yes Gender		No Gender	
	Male	Female	Male	Female	Male	Female
Newspapers	nn.n %	nn.n %	nn.n%	nn.n%	nn.n%	nn.n%
Television	nn.n	nn.n	nn.n	nn.n	nn.n	nn.n
Magazines	nn.n	nn.n	nn.n	nn.n	nn.n	nn.n
People	nn.n	nn.n	nn.n	nn.n	nn.n	nn.n
	100.0%	100.0%	100.0%	100.0%	100.0%	100.0%
	(N = nnn)	(N = nnn)	(N = nnn)	(N = nnn)	(N = nnn)	(N = nnn)
	X^2 = nn.nn, df = n p < .nn (or ns) Cramer's V = .nn		X^2 = nn.nn, df = n p < .nn (or ns) Cramer's V = .nn		X^2 = nn.nn, df = n p < .nn (or ns) Cramer's V = .nn	

* See Table 3 for comments about appropriate statistics. This format can also be used for combinations of nominal and ordinal variables or when all variables are ordinal.

Table 9   Two-way analysis of variance of gender and voting history on knowledge about the election

Main effects and interaction	Knowledge about the election*				
	Mean	SD	F	df	Significance
Main effect of gender			n.nn	n,nnn	p < .nn (or ns)
Male	n.nn	n.nn			
Female	n.nn	n.nn			
Main effect of whether person voted in 2004 election			n.nn	n,nnn	p < .nn (or ns)
Yes	n.nn	n.nn			
No	n.nn	n.nn			
Interaction between gender and voting in 2004			n.nn	n,nnn	p < .nn (or ns)
Male and Yes	n.nn	n.nn			
Male and No	n.nn	n.nn			
Female and Yes	n.nn	n.nn			
Female and No	n.nn	n.nn			

* Number of correct answers, ranging from 0 to 10.
a. $p < .05$.
b. $p < .01$.
c. $p < .001$.
Note: Where appropriate, such tables should include post hoc tests of difference between each pair of means, such as Bonferoni or Sheffei.

Figure 1   Two-way analysis of variance of gender and voting history on knowledge about the election

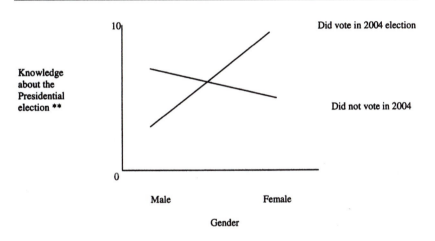

Main effect of gender :   F = *n.nn*, df = *n,nnn*, p < *.nn (or ns)*

Main effect of vote history: F = *n.nn*, df = *n,nnn*, p < *.nn (or ns)*

Interaction of gender by vote history: F = *n.nn* df = *n,nnn*, p < *.nn (or ns)*

Table 10   Analysis of covariance (age and TV news exposure) of gender and voting history on knowledge about the election

Main effects and interaction	Knowledge about the election*				
	Mean	SD	F	df	Significance
Covariates					
Age	—	—	n.nn	n,nnn	$p < .nn$ (or *ns*)
TV news exposure**	—	—	n.nn	n,nnn	$p < .nn$ (or *ns*)
Factors					
Main effect of gender			n.nn	n,nnn	$p < .nn$ (or *ns*)
Male	n.nn	n.nn			
Female	n.nn	n.nn			
Main effect of whether person voted in 2004 election			n.nn	n,nnn	$p < .nn$ (or *ns*)
Yes	n.nn	n.nn			
No	n.nn	n.nn			
Interaction between gender and voting in 2004			n.nn	n,nnn	$p < .nn$ (or *ns*)
Male and Yes	n.nn	n.nn			
Male and No	n.nn	n.nn			
Female and Yes	n.nn	n.nn			
Female and No	n.nn	n.nn			

* Number of correct answers, ranging from 0 to 10.
** "On the average, how many days a week do you watch national TV news?"
a. $p < .05$.
b. $p < .01$.
c. $p < .001$.

Table 11   Partial correlation coefficients for election knowledge by media exposure, controlling for education and income, N = nnn

Variables correlated with election knowledge**	Control variables	Zero-order correlation coefficient	Partial correlation coefficient
Newspaper exposure*		.nn^c	
	Education***		.nn^a
	Income****		.nn
	Educ, income		.nn
Local TV news exposure*		.nn^c	
	Education***		.nn^a
	Income****		.nn
	Educ, income		.nn
Local TV news exposure*		.nn^c	
	Education***		.nn^a
	Income****		.nn
	Educ, income		.nn

* Responses were coded from 0 to 7 days a week.
** Number of correct answers, ranging from 0 to 10.
*** Coded in years.
**** 1 = $10,000 or under; 2 = $20,000 to 29,999; 3 = #30,000 to 39,999; 4 = $40,000 to 49,999; 5 = $50,000 to 59,999; 6 = $60,000 to 69,999; 7 = $70,000 to 79,999; 8 = $80,000 to 80,999; 9 = $90,000 or more.
a. $p < .05$.
b. $p < .01$.
c. $p < .001$.

Table 12   Hierarchical regression analysis of demographic variables, likelihood to vote, and media use on election knowledge, N = nnn

Blocks of independent variables	Std. beta	R^2 change	Total R^2	Adjusted R^2
1. Demographic variables				
—Age	.nn[a]			
—Education	.nn			
—Income	.nn[c]			
—Gender (female = 1)	.nn	.nn[b]	.nn[b]	.nn
2. Likelihood to vote	.nn	.nn	.nn[b]	.nn
3. Whether voted in last election	.nn	.nn	.nn[b]	.nn
4. Media exposure variables				
—Newspaper	.nn[a]			
—Local TV news	.nn			
—National TV news	.nn[a]	.nn	.nn[a]	.nn

a. $p < .05$.

b. $p < .01$.

c. $p < .001$.

Table 13   Factor analysis (principal components analysis and varimax rotation) of measures of political legitimacy.

Variables	Factor 1 Evaluation	Factor 2 Legality	Factor 3 Viability	Factor 4 Stability
How subjects like the group	**.nn**	.nn	.nn	.nn
Agree with group's goals	**.nn**	.nn	.nn	.nn
Confidence it will do the right thing	**.nn**	.nn	.nn	.nn
Value to the U.S.	**.nn**	.nn	.nn	.nn
Right to exist	.nn	**.nn**	.nn	.nn
Reference system, standards	.nn	**.nn**	.nn	.nn
Peaceful/violent nature	.nn	**.nn**	.nn	.nn
Respect for law	.nn	**.nn**	.nn	.nn
Right to exercise power	.nn	**.nn**	.nn	.nn
Achieve goals	.nn	.nn	**.nn**	.nn
Similarity to traditional groups	.nn	.nn	**.nn**	.nn
Competence of the group	.nn	.nn	**.nn**	.nn
Morality of the group	.nn	.nn	**.nn**	.nn
Number of members mobilized	.nn	.nn	**.nn**	**.nn**
Financial support	.nn	.nn	**.nn**	**.nn**
Degree of organization	.nn	.nn	**.nn**	**.nn**
Fairness or exploitation	.nn	.nn	.nn	**.nn**
Stability	.nn	.nn	.nn	**.nn**
Routine nature of activities	.nn	.nn	.nn	**.nn**
Cooperation with other groups	.nn	.nn	.nn	**.nn**
Eigenvalues	n.nn	n.nn	n.nn	n.nn
% of total variance accounted for	nn.nn	nn.nn	n.nn	n.nn

Appendix B

❖ ACCEPTABLE LEVELS OF
   MEASUREMENT FOR VARIOUS STATISTICS

"x" indicates that either the "independent" or the "dependent" variable can be of this level.

"A" indicates that the "grouping" or "factor" variable can be of this level.

"B" indicates that the variable on which means are calculated can be of this level.

Statistic	Nominal	Ordinal	Interval/Ratio
Mode	x	x	x
Median		x	x
Mean			x
Range		x	x
Variance			x
Standard deviation			x
Independent t test	A*	A*	x*
Correlated/paired t test			x
F	A	A	x
X^2	x	x	x**
Cramer's V	x	x	x**
Phi	x	x	x**
Lambda	x	x	x**
Uncertainty coefficient	x	x	x**
Contingency coefficient	x	x	x**
Somers's D		x	x**
Kendall's tau b		x	x**
Kendall's tau c		x	x**
Gamma		x	x**
Spearman's rho		x	
Pearson's r			x

(Continued)

Appendix B (Continued)

Statistic	Nominal	Ordinal	Interval/Ratio
Partial r			x
Eta	A		B
Beta			x***
R			x***
R^2			x***
R^2 change			x***

*The "grouping" variable must have only two categories.

**Caution: Using this statistic with a variable of this level may be inappropriate because of the potentially large number of values in some interval- and ratio-level variables. If both variables are of interval and/or ratio level, you should probably use Pearson's r, partial r, or the regression statistics (beta, R, $R2$).

***Logit and probit regression techniques permit the use of nominal and ordinal variables as dependent. In any regression technique, nominal or ordinal variables may be dummy coded and used as independent.

References

Adams, J. L. (1979). *Conceptual blockbusting: A guide to better ideas* (2nd ed.). Stanford, CA: Stanford Alumni Association.

Adler, R. B., & Towne, N. (1990). *Looking out/looking in: Interpersonal communication* (6th ed.). Fort Worth, TX: Holt, Rinehart & Winston.

Agnew, N. M., & Pyke, S. W. (1978). *The science game: An introduction to research in the behavioral sciences* (2nd ed.). Englewood Cliffs, NJ: Prentice Hall.

Arthur, B. W. (1990). Positive feedbacks in the economy. *Scientific American, 263*, 92-99.

Aspin, D. (1984). Metaphor and meaning in educational discourse. In W. Taylor (Ed.), *Metaphors of education* (pp. 21-37). London: Heinemann Educational Books.

Axelrod, R. (1973). Schema theory: An information processing model of perception and cognition. *American Political Science Review, 67*, 1248-1266.

Babbie, E. (1998). *The practice of social research* (8th ed.). Belmont, CA: Wadsworth.

Bandura, A. (1997). *Self-efficacy: The exercise of control.* New York: W. H. Freeman.

Baran, S. J., & Davis, D. K. (1995). *Mass communication theory: Foundations, ferment and future.* Belmont, CA: Wadsworth.

Bavelas, J. (1987). Permitting creativity in science. In D. N. Jackson & J. P. Rushton (Eds.), *Scientific excellence: Origins and assessment* (pp. 307-327). Beverly Hills, CA: Sage.

Berko, R. M., Wolvin, A. D., & Wolvin, D. R. (1992). *Communicating: A social and career focus* (5th ed.). Dallas, TX: Houghton Mifflin.

Beveridge, W. I. B. (1957). *The art of scientific investigation.* New York: Vintage.

Bill, J. A., & Hardgrave, R. L., Jr. (1973). *Comparative politics: The quest for theory.* Columbus, OH: Charles E. Merrill.

Blalock, H. M., Jr. (1964). *Causal inferences in nonexperimental research.* Chapel Hill: University of North Carolina Press.

Blalock, H. M., Jr. (1969). *Theory construction: From verbal to mathematical formulations.* Englewood Cliffs, NJ: Prentice Hall.

Braddock, R. (1958). An extension of the "Lasswell formula." *Journal of Communication, 8*, 88-93.

Brown, R. (1958). *Words and things.* New York: Free Press.

Burgoon, J. K., & Buller, D. B. (1996). Reflections on the nature of theory building and the theoretical status of interpersonal deception theory. *Communication Theory, 6,* 311-328.

Cameron, J. (1992). *The artist's way: A spiritual path to higher creativity.* New York: Putnam.

Campbell, D. T., & Fiske, D. W. (1959). Convergent and discriminant validation by the multitrait-multimethod matrix. *Psychological Bulletin, 56,* 81-105.

Campbell, D. T., & Stanley, J. C. (1963). *Experimental and quasi-experimental designs for research.* Chicago: Rand McNally.

Carey, J. (1975). A cultural approach to communication. *Communication, 2,* 1-22.

Chaffee, S. H. (1977). Mass media effects: New research perspectives. In D. Lerner & L. M. Nelson (Eds.), *Communication research: A half-century appraisal* (pp. 210-241). Honolulu: University Press of Hawaii.

Chaffee, S., Zhao, X., & Leshner, G. (1994). Political knowledge and the campaign media of 1992. *Communication Research, 21,* 305-324.

Chaiken, S. (1987). The heuristic model of persuasion. In M. P. Zanna, J. M. Olson, & C. P. Herman (Eds.), *The Ontario Symposium: Social influence* (Vol. 5, pp. 3-39). Hillsdale, NJ: Lawrence Erlbaum.

Chamberlin, T. C. (1965). The method of multiple working hypotheses. *Science 148,* 754-759. (Original work published 1890)

Cohen, D. (1977). *Psychologists on psychology.* London: Routledge & Kegan Paul.

Cohen, M. R., & Nagel, E. (1934). *An introduction to logic and scientific method.* New York: Harcourt, Brace & World.

Comstock, G., & Paik, H. (1991). *Television and the American child.* San Diego, CA: Academic Press.

Comstock, G., Chaffee, S., Katzman, N., McCombs, M., & Roberts, D. (1978). *Television and human behavior.* New York: Columbia University Press.

De Bono, E. (1968). *New think: The use of lateral thinking in the generation of new ideas.* New York: Basic Books.

De Bono, E. (1992). *Serious creativity: Using the power of lateral thinking to create new ideas.* New York: Harper Collins.

DeCarufel, A. C. (1976). Research methods and the future. In L. H. Strickland, F. E. Aboud, & K. J. Gergen (Eds.), *Social psychology in transition* (pp. 335-346). New York: Plenum.

DeFleur, M. L. (1970). *Theories of mass communication.* New York: David McKay.

Deutsch, K. W. (1952). On communication models in the social sciences. *Public Opinion Quarterly, 16,* 356-380.

Dubin, R. (1978). *Theory building* (Rev. ed.). New York: Free Press.

Duncan, O. D. (1966). Path analysis: Sociological examples. *American Journal of Sociology, 72,* 1-16.

Durkheim, E. (1951). *Suicide* (J. A. Spaulding & G. Simpson, Trans.). New York: Free Press. (Original work published 1897)

Eisenberg, A. (1992, May). Metaphor in the language of science. *Scientific American, 266,*144.

Ericson, R. V., Baranak, P. M., & Chan, J. B. L. (1987). *Visualizing deviance.* Toronto: University of Toronto Press.

Eveland, W. P. (1997). Interactions and nonlinearity in mass communication: Connecting theory and methodology. *Journalism and Mass Communication Quarterly, 74,* 400-416.

Galtung, J., & Ruge, M. H. (1965). The structure of foreign news: The presentation of the Congo, Cuba and Cyprus crises in four foreign newspapers. *Journal of International Peace Research, 1,* 64-90.

Gerbner, G., & Gross, L. (1976). Living with television: The violence profile. *Journal of Communication, 26*(2), 173-199.

Gerbner, G., Gross, L., Morgan, M., & Signorielli, N. (1980). The "mainstreaming" of America: Violence profile No. 11. *Journal of Communication, 30*(3), 10-29.

Gerbner, G., Gross, L., Morgan, M., & Signorielli, N. (1986). Living with television: The dynamics of the cultivation process. In J. Bryant & C. Zillmann (Eds.), *Perspectives on media effects* (pp. 17-40). Hillsdale, NJ: Lawrence Erlbaum.

Gerbner, G., Gross, L., Morgan, M., & Signorielli, N. (1994). Growing up with television: The cultivation perspective. In J. Bryant & C. Zillmann (Eds.), *Media effects: Advances in theory and research* (pp. 17-41). Hillsdale, NJ: Lawrence Erlbaum.

Gleick, J. (1987). *Chaos: Making of a new science.* New York: Penguin.

Gould, S. J. (April, 1988). Pretty pebbles. *Natural History, 97,* 14-26.

Gowin, B. D. (1981). Philosophy. In N. L. Smith (Ed.), *Metaphors for evaluation: Sources of new methods* (pp. 181-209). Beverly Hills, CA: Sage.

Graber, D. A. (1984). *Processing the news: How people tame the information tide.* New York: Longman.

Grandmont, J. M. (1985). On endogenous competitive business cycles. *Econometrica 53,* 995-1045.

Hage, J. (1972). *Techniques and problems of theory construction in sociology.* New York: John Wiley.

Hall, S. (1980). Encoding, decoding in the television discourse. In S. Hall, D. Hobson, & P. Lowe (Eds.), *Culture, media, language.* London: Hutchinson.

Hanneman, R. A. (1988). *Computer-assisted theory building: Modeling dynamic social systems.* Newbury Park, CA: Sage.

Harvey, D. L., & Reed, M. (1996). Social science as the study of complex systems. In L. D. Kiel & E. Elliott (Eds.), *Chaos theory in the social sciences: Foundations and applications* (pp. 295-323). Ann Arbor: University of Michigan Press.

Hill, D. B. (1985). Viewer characteristics and agenda setting by television news. *Public Opinion Quarterly, 49,* 340-350.

Hirschi, T., & Selvin, H. C. (1967). *Delinquency research: An appraisal of analytic methods.* New York: Free Press.

Hoffman, R. R. (1985). Some implications of metaphor for philosophy and psychology of science. In W. Paprotte & R. Dirven (Eds.), *The ubiquity of metaphor: Metaphor in language and thought* (pp. 327-380). Amsterdam: John Benjamins.

Holmes, M. E., & Hundley, H. L. (1997). *Visualizing communication for the basic course: Narrative and conceptual patterns in textbook communication designs.* Paper presented at the Conference on Visual Communication, Jackson Hole, WY.

Holsti, O. (1969). *Content analysis for the social sciences and humanities.* Reading, MA: Addison-Wesley.

Hovland, C. I., Janis, I. L., & Kelley, H. H. (1953). *Communication and persuasion: Psychological studies of opinion change.* New Haven, CT: Yale University Press.

Hovland, C. I., Lumsdaine, A. A., & Sheffield, F. D. (1949). *Experiments in mass communication.* New York: John Wiley.

Huckfeldt, R. R. (1990). Structure, indeterminacy and chaos: A case for sociological law. *Journal of Theoretical Politics 2*, 413-433.

Hyman, H. (1955). *Survey design and analysis: Principles, cases and procedures.* Glencoe, IL: Free Press.

Kaplan, A. (1964a). *The conduct of inquiry: Methodology for behavioral science.* San Francisco: Chandler.

Kaplan, A. (1964b). *The conduct of inquiry: Methodology for behavioral science.* New York: Harper & Row.

"Kekule von Stradonitz, (Friedrich) August." (1998). *Britannica Online 1998.* Retrieved November 6, 1998, from www.eb.com:180/cgi-bin/g?DocF=micro/316/79.html.

Kendall, Patricia L., & Lazarsfeld, P. F. (1950). Problems of survey analysis. In R. K. Merton & P. F. Lazarsfeld (Eds.), *Continuities in social research* (pp. 133-196). New York: Free Press.

Kiel, L. D., & Elliott, E. (1996). *Chaos theory in the social sciences: Foundations and applications.* Ann Arbor: University of Michigan Press.

Klapper, J. T. (1960). *The effects of mass communication.* New York: Free Press.

Klijn, M. E. (1998). *The depiction of violence in Dutch and American TV news: Measuring the emphasis on comprehension or attention features in TV news of public and private media organizations.* Unpublished doctoral dissertation, University of Texas at Austin.

Kress, G. R., & van Leeuwen, T. (1996). *Reading images: The grammar of visual design.* New York: Routledge.

Krippendorff, K. (1986). *Content analysis: An introduction to its methodology.* Newbury Park, CA: Sage.

Kuhn, T. S. (1962). *The structure of scientific revolutions.* Chicago: University of Chicago Press.

Kuhn, T. S. (1970). *The structure of scientific revolutions* (2nd ed.). Chicago: University of Chicago Press.

Kulka, R. A. (1982). Idiosyncrasy and circumstances: Choices and constraints in the research process. In J. E. McGrath, J. Martin, & R. A. Kulka (Eds.), *Judgment calls in research* (pp. 41-68). Beverly Hills, CA: Sage.

Lasswell, H. D. (1948). The structure and function of communication in society. In L. Bryson (Ed.), *The communication of ideas* (pp. 117-130). New York: Harper & Bros.

Lasswell, H. D. (1960). The structure and function of communication in society. In W. Schramm (Ed.), *Mass communications* (pp. 117-130). Urbana: University of Illinois Press.

Lazarsfeld, P. F. (1955a). Foreword. In H. Hyman (Ed.), *Survey design and analysis: Principles, cases and procedures.* Glencoe, IL: Free Press.

Lazarsfeld, P. F. (1955b). Interpretation of statistical relations as a research operation. In P. F. Lazarsfeld & M. Rosenberg (Eds.), *The language of social research: A reader in the methodology of social research* (pp. 115-125). Glencoe, IL: Free Press.

Lazarsfeld, P. F., Pasanella, A. K., & Rosenberg, M. (1972). *Continuities in the language of social research.* New York: Free Press.

Lieberson, S. (1985). *Making it count: The improvement of social research and theory.* Berkeley: University of California Press.

Littlejohn, S. W. (1983). *Theories of human communication.* Belmont, CA: Wadsworth.

Lowden, N., Andersen, P., Dozier, D., & Lauzen, M. (1994). Media use in the primary election: A secondary medium model. *Communication Research, 21,* 293-304.

MacCormac, E. R. (1976). *Metaphor and myth in science and religion.* Durham, NC: Duke University Press.

Martin, J. (1982). A garbage can model of the research process. In J. E. McGrath, J. Martin, & R. A. Kulka (Eds.), *Judgment calls in research* (pp. 17-39). Beverly Hills, CA: Sage.

McCombs, M. E. (1981). The agenda-setting approach. In D. D. Nimmo & K. R. Sanders (Eds.), *Handbook of political communication* (pp. 121-140). Beverly Hills, CA: Sage.

McCombs, M. E., & Shaw, D. L. (1972). The agenda-setting function of mass media. *Public Opinion Quarterly, 36,* 176-187.

McCombs, M. E., & Becker, L. B. (1979). *Using mass communication theory.* Englewood Cliffs, NJ: Prentice Hall.

McCombs, M. E., & Shaw, D. L. (1977). The agenda-setting function of the press. In D. L. Shaw & M. E. McCombs (Eds.), *The emergence of American political issues: The agenda-setting function of the press* (pp. 1-18). St. Paul, MN: West.

McGrath, J. E. (1982). Dilemmatics: The study of research choices and dilemmas. In J. E. McGrath, J. Martin, & R. A. Kulka (Eds.), *Judgment calls in research* (pp. 69-102). Beverly Hills, CA: Sage.

McGuire, W. J. (1968). Personality and attitude change: An information-processing theory. In A. C. Greenwald, T. C. Brock, & T. M. Ostrom (Eds.),

Psychological foundations of attitudes (pp. 171-196). San Diego, CA: Academic Press.

McGuire, W. (1973). The yin and yang of progress in social psychology: Seven koan. *Journal of Personality and Social Psychology, 26,* 446-456.

McGuire, W. J. (1976). The yin and yang of progress in social psychology: Seven koan. In L. H. Strickland, F. E. Aboud, & K. J. Gergen (Eds.), *Social psychology in transition* (pp. 33-49). New York: Plenum.

McGuire, W. J. (1981). Theoretical foundations of campaigns. In R. E. Rice & W. J. Paisley (Eds.), *Public communication campaigns* (pp. 41-70). Beverly Hills, CA: Sage.

McGuire, W., & Papageorgis, D. (1961). The relative efficacy of various types of prior belief-defense in producing immunity against persuasion. *Journal of Abnormal and Social Psychology, 62,* 327-337.

McLeod, J., Daily, K., Guo, Z., Eveland, Jr., W., Bayer, J., Yang, S., & Wang, H. (1996). Community integration, local media use, and democratic processes. *Communication Research, 23*(2), 179-209.

McQuail, D. (1994). *Mass communication theory: An introduction* (3rd ed.). Thousand Oaks, CA: Sage.

McQuail, D., & Windahl, S. (1993). *Communication models for the study of mass communication* (2nd ed.). London: Longman.

Meadow, R. G. (1985). Political communication research in the 1980s. *Journal of Communication, 35*(1), 157-173.

Merriam-Webster Dictionary online. (2003). Retrieved Sept. 6, 2003, from www.m-w.com/cgi-bin/dictionary.

Merton, R. K. (1957). *Social theory and social structure.* Glencoe, IL: Free Press.

Miller, J. G. (1955). Toward a general theory for the behavioral sciences. *American Psychologist, 10,* 513-531.

Miller, J. G. (1995). *Living systems.* Niwot, CO: University Press of Colorado.

National Television Violence Study. (1996). Studio City, CA.: Mediascope.

Neuliep, J. W. (1996). *Human communication theory: Applications and case studies.* Boston: Allyn & Bacon.

Noelle-Neumann, E. (1993). *The spiral of silence: Public opinion—our social skin* (2nd ed.). Chicago: University of Chicago Press.

O'Keefe, G. J. (1985). "Taking a bite out of crime": The impact of a public information campaign. *Communication Research, 12,* 147-178.

Osborn, A. F. (1963). *Applied imagination: Principles and procedures of creative problem-solving* (3rd ed.). New York: Scribner.

Oxford English Dictionary Online. (2003). Retrieved Sept. 6, 2003, from http://dictionary.oed.com/cgi/entry/00053536?single=1&query_type=w ord&queryword=creativity&edition=2e&first=1&max_to_show=10.

Petty, R. E., & Cacioppo, J. T. (1981). *Attitudes and persuasion: Classic and contemporary approaches.* Dubuque, IA: Wm. C. Brown.

Platt, J. R. (1962). *The excitement of science.* Boston: Houghton Mifflin.

Platt, J. R. (1964, October 16). Strong inference. *Science, 146,* 347-353.

Poincaré, H. (1952). Mathematical creation. In B. Ghiselin (Ed.), *The creative process* (pp. 33-42). New York: New American Library.

Popper, K. (1959). *The logic of scientific discovery.* New York: Harper & Row.

Popper, K. R. (1965a). *Conjectures and refutations: The growth of scientific knowledge.* New York: Harper & Row.

Popper, K. (1965b). *The logic of scientific discovery* (2nd ed.). New York: Harper & Row.

Popper, K. (1968). *The logic of scientific discovery* (3rd, Rev. ed.). New York: Harper & Row.

Popper, K. (1972). *Objective knowledge.* Oxford, UK: Clarendon.

Prigogine, I., & Stengers, I. (1984). *Order out of chaos: Man's new dialogue with nature.* New York: Bantam.

Rosenberg, M. (1968). *The logic of survey analysis.* New York: Basic Books.

Saperstein, A. M., & Mayer-Kress, G. (1989). A non-linear dynamical model of the impact of S.D.I. on the arms race. *Journal of Conflict Resolution 35,* 636-670.

Schramm, W. (1954). How communication works. In W. Schramm (Ed.), *The process and effects of mass communication.* Urbana: University of Illinois Press.

Schramm, W. (1961). How communication works. In W. Schramm (Ed.), *The process and effects of mass communication* (2nd ed., pp. 3-26). Urbana, IL: University of Illinois Press.

Schramm, W. (1964). *Mass media and national development: The role of information in the developing countries.* Stanford, CA: Stanford University Press.

Schramm, W. (1971). The nature of communication between humans. In W. Schramm & D. F. Roberts (Eds.), *The process and effects of mass communication* (Rev. ed., pp. 3-53). Urbana: University of Illinois Press.

Schramm, W., Lyle, J., & Parker, E. B. (1961). *Television in the lives of our children.* Stanford, CA: Stanford University Press.

Severin, W. J., & Tankard, J. W. (1997). *Communication theories: Origins, methods, and uses in the mass media* (4th ed.). New York: Longman.

Severin, W. J., & Tankard, J. W. (2001). *Communication theories: Origins, methods, and uses in the mass media* (5th ed.). New York: Longman.

Shannon, C. E., & Weaver, W. (1949). *The mathematical theory of communication.* Urbana: University of Illinois Press.

Shaw, D. L., & McCombs, M. E. (1977). *The emergence of American political issues: The agenda-setting function of the press.* St. Paul, MN: West.

Shoemaker, P. (1984). Media treatment of deviant political groups. *Journalism Quarterly, 61*(1), 66-75, 82.

Shoemaker, P. J. (1991). *Gatekeeping.* Newbury Park, CA: Sage.

Shoemaker, P. (1996). Hard-wired for news: Using biological and cultural evolution to explain the news. *Journal of Communication, 46,* 32-47.

Shoemaker, P. J., & Reese, S. D. (1996). *Mediating the message: Theories of influences on mass media content* (2nd ed.). White Plains, NY: Longman.

Shoemaker, P., Wanta, W., & Leggett, D. (1989). Drug coverage and public opinion, 1972-1986. In P. Shoemaker (Ed.), *Communication campaigns about drugs: Government, media and the public* (pp. 67-80). Hillsdale, NJ: Lawrence Erlbaum.

Stinchcomb, A. L. (1968). *Constructing social theories.* New York: Harcourt, Brace & World.

Suplee, C. (2000, July 20). The speed of light is exceeded in lab. *Washington Post,* p. A1.

Tankard, J. W. (1994). Visual crosstabs: A technique for enriching information graphics. *Mass Communication Review 21*(1 & 2), 49-66.

Thorngate, W. (1976). Possible limits on a science of social behavior. In L. H. Strickland, F. E. Aboud, & K. J. Gergen (Eds.), *Social psychology in transition* (pp. 121-139). New York: Plenum.

Tichenor, P., Donohue, G., & Olien, C. (1970). Mass media flow and differential growth in knowledge. *Public Opinion Quarterly, 34,* 158-170.

Wallace, W. A. (1994). *Ethics in modeling.* Tarrytown, NY: Elsevier Science.

Watson, J. D. (1968). *The double helix: A personal account of the discovery of the structure of DNA.* New York: Atheneum.

Webster's New World Dictionary. (1962). New York: World Publishing.

Westley, B. H., & MacLean, M. (1957). A conceptual model for communication research. *Journalism Quarterly, 34,* 31-38.

Winter, J. P. (1981). Contingent conditions in the agenda-setting process. In G. C. Wilhoit & H. de Bock (Eds.), *Mass communication review yearbook* (Vol. 2, pp. 235-243). Beverly Hills, CA: Sage.

Wright, S. (1921). Correlation and causation. *Journal of Agricultural Research, 20,* 557-585.

Young, T. R. (1991). Change and chaos theory: Metaphysics of the postmodern. *Social Science Journal, 28,* 289-305.

Zucker, H. G. (1978). The variable nature of news media influence. In B. D. Ruben (Ed.), *Communication yearbook* (Vol. 2, pp. 225-240). New Brunswick, NJ: Transaction.

Index

About the Authors

Dominic L. Lasorsa is an Associate Professor of Journalism at the University of Texas at Austin. He received a BA in journalism from St. Bonaventure University, an MA in journalism from the University of Texas at Austin, and a PhD in communication from Stanford University. In college, he served as editor-in-chief of his school newspaper, the *Bonaventure,* and worked at the *Suffolk (N.Y.) Sun* as a Dow Jones Newspaper Fund Editing Intern. Upon graduation, he entered the U.S. Air Force, where he served as a Radio Communications Specialist and a Curriculum Development Specialist. He then worked as a reporter and editor at the *Wichita (Kansas) Eagle* and the *Austin (Texas) American-Statesman.* Before beginning his academic career, he served as editor-in-chief of the *Marble Falls (Texas) Highlander.* He studies and teaches communication theory and methods, focusing on political communication and media effects. He has published articles in numerous books, journals, and other publications. His works have appeared in the *Encyclopedia of International Media and Communications,* the *Historical Dictionary of Political Communication in the United States,* the *International Journal of Public Opinion Research,* the *Journal of Communication,* the *Journal of Media Economics,* the *Journal of Reading,* the *Journalism and Mass Communication Quarterly, Journalism Studies,* and the *Newspaper Research Journal.* He was a co-author of the three-volume *National Television Violence Study.*

Pamela J. Shoemaker (PhD, Wisconsin-Madison) is the John Ben Snow Professor in the S. I. Newhouse School of Public Communications at Syracuse University. Her research chair is devoted to the study of news, and she has recently completed a 10-country study on the definition of news across cultures, building and testing her own theory. She is the coeditor of *Communication Research,* a top social science communication journal. She is also the coauthor of *Mediating the Message: Theories of Influences on Mass Media Content,* author of *Gatekeeping,* and editor of

Communication Campaigns About Drugs: Government, Media, Public. She is Past-President of the Association for Education in Journalism and Mass Communication and Chair of the Mass Communication Division of the International Communication Association. She teaches courses in social science research methods and statistics, as well as theory. At this writing, she has lectured in 16 countries.

James W. Tankard, Jr., is the Jesse H. Jones Professor in Journalism at the University of Texas at Austin. He was born in Newport News, Va. He attended Virginia Tech, where he was coeditor of the student newspaper and received a BS in general science. He received a master's of journalism degree from the University of North Carolina and a PhD in communication from Stanford University. He has worked for the Associated Press in Charlotte, N.C., and for the *Raleigh Times* as a county government reporter. He has also held summer jobs and other short-term positions with the Newport News (Va.) *Daily Press*, the U.S. Information Agency, and the Lampasas (Texas) *Dispatch and Record*. He has taught journalism at the University of Wisconsin, Temple University, and the University of Texas at Austin. He taught one of the first classes in the Senior Fellows Program, the honors program within the College of Communication at the University of Texas. He served for 6 years as the editor of *Journalism Monographs*. He is the author of *The Statistical Pioneers*, the coauthor of *Basic News Reporting* (with Michael Ryan), and the coauthor of *Communication Theories* (with Werner Severin). The latter is in its fifth edition and has been translated into five languages.